Title: Dusk
Artist: Carl Lavoie

Title: Night
Artist: Carl Lavoie

Vastarien

A Literary Journal

Issue One

Matt Cardin and Jon Padgett, Co-Editors-In Chief

Dagny Paul, Senior Editor

New Orleans, Louisiana

© 2018 Grimscribe Press

Cover art by Dave Felton

Cover design by Anna Trueman

All rights reserved. No part of this publication may be reproduced, distributed, or transmitted in any form or by any means, including photocopying, recording, or other electronic or mechanical methods, without the prior written permission of the publisher, except in the case of brief quotations embodied in critical reviews and certain other noncommercial uses permitted by copyright law.

Published by

Grimscribe Press
New Orleans, LA
USA

https://vastarien-journal.com

To Tom and the members of TLO

CONTENTS

Acknowledgments   i

Foreword to the Polish edition of *Teatro Grottesco* (*Okultura*, 2014)   1
Thomas Ligotti

The Gods in Their Seats, Unblinking   7
Kurt Fawver

The Nightmare of His Art: The Horrific Power of the Imagination in "The Troubles of Dr. Thoss" and "Gas Station Carnivals"   31
W. Silverwood

Affirmation of the Spirit: Consciousness, Transformation, and the Fourth World in Film   49
Christopher Slatsky

Try the Veal   63
Robert Beveridge

How to Construct a Gun from Your Own Flesh   65
Michael Uhall

"Eccentric to the Healthy Social Order": Inversions of Family, Community, and Religion in Thomas Ligotti's The Last Feast of Harlequin   71
Michael J. Abolafia

"They say I should kill myself and not try to spoil their enjoyment in being alive": An Interview with Thomas Ligotti   83
Wojciech Gunia

Wraiths   91
Wade German

Eraserhead as Antinatalist Allegory   93
Colby Smith

The Theatre of Ovid *Aaron Worth*	107
The Alienation of the Self: Marx, Polanyi, and Ligottian Horror *S. L. Edwards*	129
Strange Bird *Ian Mullins*	139
Solar Flare *Paul L. Bates*	141
Night Walks: The Films of Val Lewton *Michael Penkas*	149
Infinite Light, Infinite Darkness *Martin Rose*	169
Nervous Wares & Abnormal Stares *Devin Goff*	187
My Time at the Drake Clinic *Jordan Krall*	203
Notes on a Horror *Dr. Raymond Thoss*	217
Singing the Song of My Unmaking *Christopher Ropes*	241
Contributors	259

ACKNOWLEDGMENTS

Many thanks to Kevin Moquin and Shawn Mann for conceiving of a Ligotti-related literary journal and providing invaluable planning, research and editing before they stepped away from the project. Thanks to all the members of Thomas Ligotti Online and to our benefactors, including Michael Adams, Rebecca J. Allred, Claus Appel, James Baker, Rebecca Baumann, Corey Bond, BeelzeBob, bendk, Chris Bozzone, Bret Burks, Ross T. Byers, Cadabra Records, GMarkC, Kory Callaway, Matthew Carpenter, Daniel Clanton, Zak Cowell, William DeGeest, Ivan Dehaes (Belgium), Scott Desmarais, Jason T. DiModica, Alexandra Dimou, Lee Dong-Hyun, C.P. Dunphey, Pamela Durgin, Mark Erickson, Iago Faustus, Darren Fisher, Philip Fracassi, FuFu Frauenwahl, Chris "Waffles" Gomes, A.L. Grenfell, Ariel Guzman, Zack Haskin, Fred Herman, Cameron Higby-Naquin, Kevin Holderny, Travis R. Hurst, Kai, Kostas Ikonomopoulos, Holly Iossa, Thomas W. Iverson, Jacob J., George Jack, R.A. Jamison, R. L. Joines, Zachary Knackstedt, Trent Kollodge, Andrew S Koury, James Krstulovich, Jed Lackritz, Karolina Lebek, Gavin Lees, Paul Leong, Lord Jim, Alice Maynwaring, Christopher R. Mountenay, Joseph Murray, Andrew Nevins, Alexander Nirenberg, Mark O'Neill, Mike O'Neil, Robert Osgood, Brian Poe, Todd Quinn, Niko Ranta, Kay Reeves, Will Rieder, Andrew R., Dave Roberts, A. S., David Sharp, Todd Slawsby, Justin Steele, Blaine Stevens, Brian Stevens, Lysette Stevenson, Jeremy Stuckwisch, Aron Tarbuck, Kenneth Thomas, Darren Tunseth, Benjamin Uminsky, Roger Venable, Magnus Vinstrup, Dom Voyce, Ian Walshaw, Damian Walter, Ryan Walz, Scott Wetherby, and J. P. Wiske.

Foreword to *Teatro Grottesco*
(*Okultura*, 2014)

By Thomas Ligotti

Editor's note: *This foreword first appeared in the Polish edition of Ligotti's fiction collection* Teatro Grottesco, *translated by Wojciech Gunia, Mateusz Kopacz, Filip Skutela, and Aleksander Więckowski, with help from Sławomir Wielhorski. It was written by the author specifically for that edition. This is its first publication in English.*

IN 1977 I was browsing in a bookstore and came across a slim paperback titled after one of the stories in the book *The Street of Crocodiles*. It was a reprint of a 1963 English translation of *Sklepy Cynamonowe*, a book published in 1934 by Bruno Schulz. I had not yet begun to write the stories that would later appear in my various collections. Nevertheless, I had already sketched in my imagination, as well as in some early unpublished efforts, the type of wonderfully decayed and musty small-town world that Schulz had invented decades before I was born.

Even though I was brought up in another time and place than Schulz, when it came time to most sincerely express the architecture of what might be called my soul, that time and place was of no use to me. My greatest problem as an embryonic author was finding the characters and settings that suited my imagination. The people and locales among which I was raised were foreign to me. Of course, as a citizen of the suburbs on the outskirts of a major industrial city, I was integrated body and soul (to use that word again) into my homeland much like any other person my age, though perhaps somewhat more alien than most to the society in which I maneuvered. However, when it came time to act as a creative being, I discovered that I merely lived in that environment but was not *of* it. My passport bore the stamps of other regions—not so much other national entities as other realms that encouraged the more alien, though to me more natural, aspects of my nature.

Perhaps Schulz felt the same way about his own birthplace and surroundings as I did about mine. Like me, he did not seem attached to the so-called realities of his hometown of Drogobych. The first glimpse I had of this town when I entered its streets through the medium of his book was that of a fence constructed of plain boards beneath which trickled a rivulet of foul, black water, a fetid drainage ditch of scum and mud. Somehow I knew this place, as if this back-alley image was from an old photograph album that opened up in my mind and told me the real story of my life and the history of my real home. I knew little of how mature, documented citizens lived and worked and frolicked in my country, not in any profound sense that I could describe with personal authority. And naturally I knew nothing about 1930s Drogobych either. Yet I knew that dirty little rivulet and the crummy environs through which it dribbled. Who would choose to focus on such a scene rather than a busy promenade of the kind found in every town and city of the earth, the meeting ground and showcase for those who were truly active participants in the social machinery that functions the world over? The answer was that *Schulz* would focus on such a scene. And so would I.

This much I knew during the moments I stood alone in that bookstore, stopped to look through the windows of Schulz's cinnamon shops, and wandered down Schulz's streets and even more through the alleys behind them and the empty lots around them.

Aside from a few shadowy snapshots in my nonexistent photograph album, I cannot compare my stories to those of Bruno Schulz. I am a horror writer, after all, and not a genius free to recreate the whole world, as Schulz did. In addition, before I came to inhabit the passages through Schulz's universe, I had already passed through those of H. P. Lovecraft's decayed New England towns and the cosmos that weighed down upon them like a heavy fog full of monstrous organisms one might sense but seldom see or hear. Of course, Lovecraft was fortunate enough to live within the vicinity of the real-life models of those towns. Many years later, I made a visit to those towns. I could not stay very long, though, and what I took home with me was only a memory of some towns that were nothing like those in Lovecraft's stories. I had been in them, but I was not *of* them any more than I was a true resident of my own home town, which was not even a town—just a suburb, a very nice one, so it was not the sort of place where I might come across that septic rivulet in the story by Schulz which had so captivated me. To me, such things existed only in my dreams. These were my model.

I could never traffic in the common ways of realistic fiction. That was what you were supposed to do, whether or not you were a writer of supernatural horror fiction. Still, I did my best to invent a kind of reality—an unreal reality—that was like dreams and not like them at the same time. In my study of Edgar Poe's work, I noticed that this is what he had done. Some of his stories take place in a town that can be found on a map. His best stories, however, are situated in an imaginary setting. For instance, if you found yourself on the way to the house of Usher, you could not change course and visit New York or Boston on the way there. That would be like choosing to leave one of your dreams and go on a vacation to Tahiti or London or some other place where people take vacations. No, you could only go to the house of Usher. There was no choice. The trick, of course, is to trap the reader in those dreams they cannot escape while they are reading a story.

It is not often, as we know, that one realizes one is dreaming some kind of delirious nonsense. At the same time, nothing is more real than a dream when you are caught in its boundaries. These, then, became the boundaries of my stories and the limits beyond which the characters in them could not travel. Sometimes they have names, and sometimes they are anonymous. What was the name of Schulz's Street of Crocodiles? What was my name before I was born? For me, as someone who wanted to be a writer of horror stories, what mattered in a practical sense was how these questions haunt a reader the way I was haunted by my own idols of dreams such as Schulz, Lovecraft, and Poe.

I wish I could say that my progress toward writing the stories in this book, and others like them, was as neat and efficient as I have previously described. But like most writers, I had to stumble my way down many streets before I knew where I wanted to go. Others pointed the way to me, but I had to figure out that all I had as a writer was myself. More particularly, what I had were my dreams. I am not always in my dreams . . . but I am always *of* them. I think this is true of many of us, especially those readers of horror stories who, it must be said, are rather unwholesome individuals who enjoy being haunted by things that may only happen in dreams.

Untitled
Artist: Dave Felton

The Gods in Their Seats, Unblinking

By Kurt Fawver

Publisher's Preface

THE FOLLOWING *play's debut—and only—performance was purportedly held at the Uphill Theater in Philadelphia, Pennsylvania, on April 13, 2012, as part of a minor festival of one-act performances. The part of Mr. Krill was listed as being performed by Jackson Landsdale. The part of Dr. Nazir was listed as being performed by Gabriel Torres.*

The play first emerged in public consciousness in late 2012, when Evan Elster, a virtually unknown playwright from the Philadelphia metropolitan area, posted the text of it to the comment board of a New Jersey paranormal investigation group. Elster claimed the play had "stolen away" several of his friends, including his girlfriend and sister, both of whom were struggling actresses. When further prompted to explain what he meant by "stolen away," Elster insisted that the entire audience and everyone involved in the play's production, from theater owner to stagehands, had simply vanished following its late-night debut performance.

Certain verifiable facts lend a measure of credence to Elster's claims. The Uphill Theater, now defunct, was operated by an unknown benefactor. The whereabouts of the actors involved in that one-night performance are unknown, despite a concerted effort by law enforcement officials to locate both individuals. The playwright, by all accounts, has never existed—or, at the very least, has never held any known national or organizational affiliation.

Regarding its merit as a piece of fiction, *The Gods in Their Seats, Unblinking* is certainly serviceable as a character study of paranoid delusion, but its true value lies in its wide-reaching implications concerning the nature of character and the role of audience. That it has roots in meta-textualism and postmodern conceptions of reader response does make the text more difficult to quantify, but we can easily recognize that what Zanaraya (if, indeed, the author's name is accurate) attempted in the play was to incite a creeping sense of dread, of watching and being watched. On this level, the text is also relatively successful, as Krill's detachment causes us to wonder if, perhaps, he sees what Nazir cannot and, in turn, what we cannot.

We present the text here exactly as it was posted online by Elster, without alteration. Presumably this is also the text as it was performed in Philadelphia, if indeed the performance took place.

The Gods in Their Seats, Unblinking

A single-act drama by
S. K. Zanaraya

Dramatis Personae

MR. KRILL – a psychiatric inpatient
DR. NAZIR – a physician at Krill's care facility

Interior of DR. NAZIR's office, side view. Walls are missing, replaced with slabs of darkness. Illumination is dim, barely more than twilight. The few furnishings in the room are ornate, bordering on the Gothic: the doctor's desk—a tremendous, carved hunk of dark oak, the doctor's chair—a black, high-backed leather throne, and two chairs for guests—both deeply padded and upholstered in crimson silk. On the doctor's desk rests a panoply of medical and office equipment as well as a forest of stacked books, many of which are ornately cloth-bound and heavily foxed.

KRILL sits one of the silk chairs, alone, facing NAZIR's cluttered desk. His head is turned toward the audience, his eyes darting between theatergoers, attempting to take in the entirety of the house. KRILL's countenance is one of sublime recognition, as though he is forced to live in a place eternally pressed between terror and wonder. During the entire duration of the play, KRILL's gaze never leaves the audience.

NAZIR enters, smiling and carrying a tablet computer. He takes a seat at his desk opposite KRILL.

> DR. NAZIR

Mr. Krill, how are you this evening?

> KRILL
> (distant)

They're out there, doctor. As always. They're out there watching, listening. Right now.

> DR. NAZIR
> (consults his tablet)

Well, your vitals are looking good, I can say that much.
> (a pause)

How do you feel? Any new experiences?

> KRILL

Out in that place, whatever it is. Always waiting for us. Always seeing this one moment.

DR. NAZIR

The same one?

KRILL

The same one.

DR. NAZIR

So you're still suffering from selective amnesia, then. What about the hallucinations?

KRILL
(sits upright, suddenly intense, agitated)

What makes a thing *real*, doctor? Observation. We exist because *they* see us and hear us. We exist because *they're* interested in watching us *do* things and *be* things.

NAZIR lays his tablet on his desk and stares at KRILL. He nods, slowly.

DR. NAZIR

Fine, Mr. Krill. If that's what you really want to do today. Let's explore your theory yet again. Let's assume, for the moment, that you're right. Another dimension exists alongside ours, and that within that dimension a sea of eyes and an ocean of ears are constantly watching us and listening to us.

KRILL

We don't have to assume. It's right there in front of us.

DR. NAZIR

Even if it is, Mr. Krill, ask yourself, why would these eyes and ears be watching and listening to *us* of all people? Why would they care about *you* or *me*? Why are we so special as to be studied by—what? beings? —from another reality?

KRILL

You feel it, doctor. I know you do. You feel them.

DR. NAZIR

(visibly uncomfortable)

Mr. Krill, please try to focus. Why would we be watched? Why would we be listened to?

KRILL

We're what's here, I suppose.

(a pause, a moment of consideration)

When you wake in the morning, do you have any choice as to what rushes into your vision? Do you have any control over the reality that washes up to your eyes? No. Of course not. But the things out there –

(motions with his chin toward the audience)

they do. They can *choose* to enter our world. They can *choose* to look at us or look away. They watch us because we're *here* and we've been chosen to *be* watched.

DR. NAZIR

(leaning forward in his chair)

But why wouldn't they look away? What motivates their choice to look at us? We're not particularly interesting. Certainly no more than anything or anyone else in the universe.

KRILL

(shakes his head)

We're not interesting to ourselves, maybe. But we are to them. We're not part of their reality. We're . . . different somehow.

(a pause)

And they want something from us.

NAZIR picks up a pen and grabs a piece of paper that's close at hand.

DR. NAZIR
And what is that?

KRILL opens his mouth to speak, but then closes it, slowly. He shrugs.

As KRILL begins to talk, NAZIR scribbles notes on the paper.

KRILL
I don't know. A need. A desire. All the pupils boring, sinking into my soul. They're out there. Poking. Prodding. Squeezing and reshaping and embracing me in the darkness. Reshaping and embracing you, too, doctor. It's like . . . it's like they're trying to dissect us and build us at the same time. Their eyes—like pincers, talons, steel incisors, like welding flames and thick rivets.

DR. NAZIR
So you feel that the things are . . . trying to hurt us?

KRILL
(shaking his head)
No. No. Not hurt. Not really. Unmake us. And make us. Each set of eyes, a different reconfiguration, a different mold, a different me and a different you. They cut deep so they can pull out your guts and add . . . things . . . ideas . . . feelings . . . thoughts. They stuff us full of ourselves.

> DR. NAZIR
> (still writing, distracted)

So . . . then . . . you are not you when *they're* watching?

> KRILL
> (annoyed)

I've told you before, we *only* exist when they watch. And we can only be *anything* when they make us. I'm only ever the me they want me to be.

> DR. NAZIR

And if they're not watching? Then . . . we disappear? We are nothing? Is that it, Mr. Krill?

> KRILL

Does the past disappear? Does the future ever arrive? Is there ever anything but *now*?

NAZIR drops his pen and frowns.

> DR. NAZIR
> (disappointed)

And we're back to the selective amnesia. Mr. Krill, you know that you don't disappear when you walk out of this room. You eat outside this room, sleep outside this room, watch television and read outside this room. You don't stop being when we stop talking. You're *always* here, very much a part of the world.

> KRILL

Exactly. But wrong emphasis. I'm always *here*. The world doesn't exist outside this room because *they* don't see it. This *is* the world. This is *our* world, in its entirety. You just can't recognize that yet, doctor. You feel it, but you don't recognize it.

> DR. NAZIR
> (as if trying to avoid Krill's last statement)

Wait, wait. You said they, the . . . ah . . . beings from beyond, can choose to see what they want to see. Well, why don't they choose to see what's outside this room, then?

> KRILL
> (pauses in thought, then, quietly)

You're not understanding. There is no outside. There is no inside. There's only here and now. A moment where we're all together. The eyes. The ears. Us.

KRILL stands and walks to the edge of the stage. He holds his hands out in supplication, as though offering his soul to the audience.

> KRILL

Do you believe in God, doctor?

> DR. NAZIR

I don't think that's quite germane to our conversation.

> KRILL

Because I'm not sure. But I wonder. What if? What if there is a God and It didn't mean to create anything? What if It just swivels its gaze and observes and existence appears? And what if It only has that power because of Its relation to us? Because It's outside our frame of reference?

> DR. NAZIR

If you'd like to speak to a chaplain, we have one on staff. I'm sure he's more equipped to answer these questions . . .

KRILL waves off the comment.

KRILL

What if those are the thousand eyes of God I see?

DR. NAZIR

I thought you said they were beings from another reality, Mr. Krill.

KRILL

Those ideas aren't mutually exclusive.

DR. NAZIR
(smiles nervously)

So what if those *are* the eyes of God? What then? You can see them, but I can't. Why?

KRILL shakes his head and reaches toward the audience, grabbing at air.

KRILL

I think you can, doc. Just not yet. Besides, I'm different than you.

DR. NAZIR

Different how, Mr. Krill? Are you some sort of . . . prophet?

KRILL
(shrugs)

How can I tell G-flat from G? How can you differentiate burgundy from maroon? It's just . . . how we must be, how we're . . . drawn. I'm a prophet if that's what they decide I am. I'm a nobody if that's what they decide instead. Either way, it doesn't change the fact that I can do things you can't, and you can do things I can't. They like to be able to tell us apart, after all.

>DR. NAZIR
>(suddenly writing with demonic fever)

I'm interested in a word you mentioned: drawn. Who draws us, exactly?

>KRILL
>(kicks the floor in frustration and sighs)

The eyes! The ears! They're shading us right now, applying a spectrum of grey to everything about us—the way we think, the way we feel, the things we do or might do or have done in the past. They're giving us depth, doctor. But they're cutting us into little strips to do it. Can't you feel their scalpeled minds, filleting us, paring our memories, our lives? Can you really not feel it?

NAZIR reaches for his tablet computer. He swipes at its screen with his index finger as though conducting a violent symphonic score.

>DR. NAZIR

Let's move away from this particular line of inquiry for a moment, Mr. Krill. Let's discuss these instead.

NAZIR motions to the stacks of books on his desk. He takes one from a pile, cracks open the cover, and reads the frontispiece.

>DR. NAZIR

"*The Phenomenological Manifestation of Meaning* by Athena Nevill."
>(he drops the book and picks up another, again opening the cover and reading)

"*Dioses en letras, dioses de las palabras* – Xavier Curazco."

> (he lets the book fall and grabs yet another)

"*Die Apokalypse in der Zeichensetzung: eine Theorie von Josef Leiber.*"

> (he tosses the book amongst the rest)

Interesting titles, Mr. Krill. You've been sending away for these volumes since last winter. These aren't like the books other patients receive. No *New York Times* bestsellers or blockbuster movie adaptations here. Not for you, Mr. Krill. This is complex material. Expensive material. Some of these books are over two hundred years old and quite rare. I checked.

KRILL, quite tentatively, lifts his foot out, over the edge of the stage. He draws it back immediately, a triumphant smile spreading over his face.

KRILL
> (in deep thought)

So it's possible. It's entirely possible. Once you know, once you understand. You can break it. You can break anything.

NAZIR clears his throat and slaps the books.

DR. NAZIR

Mr. Krill? Your personal library here?

KRILL

What about it? It's fiction. It's all fiction. Everything is fiction. We just choose to cling tightly to some of those fictions and call them reality.

DR. NAZIR

Is that what these books have taught you?

Again, KRILL extends his foot over the precipice. This time, he holds it in the air for a few seconds before retracting it.

KRILL

I've never read those books. They're always on your desk during this meeting. I don't know how they get there. I don't know who arranges them. I don't know what they say or what they mean.

DR. NAZIR

So you claim you've never read any of them? Even though we've discussed a great deal of their substance in previous meetings?

KRILL

We've never had any other meeting but this one.

NAZIR slides the computer to the side and jots down more notes. His pen strikes the paper with the force of a butcher hacking at a side of meat.

DR. NAZIR

The amnesia seems to be especially severe this month. I think we'll have to raise the dosage of a few of your medications.

KRILL

What if I told you that you weren't real, doctor? What if I told you the eyes and the ears out there, beyond time, beyond space,
(he motions to the audience)
are the only way you exist? What if I told you that once they close, you blink into nothing?

NAZIR smiles, seemingly amused.

DR. NAZIR

I'm not real?

KRILL

Maybe. Maybe not. Who's your favorite character from all the literature you've ever read?

DR. NAZIR

A bit off topic, Mr. Krill. But, if you'd like to know, I've always been partial to Captain Ahab.

KRILL crouches and runs his hand along the edge of the stage, his fingers splayed out into space. He angles his body so that NAZIR cannot see his actions.

KRILL

You know who I think is fascinating? Milton's Satan. He recognizes a logical inconsistency in the cosmological hierarchy, calls God on it, and is punished for his action. He sees an abuse of power and he opts out of the whole damn system, preferring to suffer the flames of hell rather than become a prisoner to heaven.

DR. NAZIR

Do you liken yourself to that character, Mr. Krill?

KRILL

Do you liken yourself to Captain Ahab?

DR. NAZIR

In some respects, yes, I'd say I do.

KRILL waggles his fingers at the audience, then hurriedly draws them back, as though expecting them to be cut off, crushed, bitten, or burned.

KRILL

So are you Captain Ahab or is Captain Ahab you? Because the difference is, pardon the pun, critical.

NAZIR sighs, drops his pen, and pushes away from the desk.

DR. NAZIR

You've been corresponding with your former colleagues, I take it? Which one of the trio? You're all in separate wards for a reason, Mr. Krill. When you see those individuals, you begin to discuss your former . . . interests.

KRILL takes several steps away from the stage's edge, seems to be judging something about the distance.

KRILL

The occult, doctor. You can say it.

DR. NAZIR

Yes, the occult. You talk with them about your master plan to "end the universe" and you begin to believe in it again. So which one did you see? Barrow? Salazar?

KRILL

Doctor, would you come here?

KRILL gestures to NAZIR to stand beside him.

KRILL

I need you to look at something.

Hesitantly, NAZIR walks to KRILL and stands where KRILL had directed.

DR. NAZIR

And what am I looking at?

KRILL points to the audience.

KRILL

What do you see there?

DR. NAZIR

A wall. A light blue wall.

KRILL

No. Look beyond it. See the eyes, doctor, the ears. Feel their instruments inside you.

DR. NAZIR

I see my medical license. I see my degree from Penn State. I see . . .

KRILL

You see what the text demands of you.

DR. NAZIR

What text is that? The one the . . . ah . . . the eyes and ears of God have written? Is that right?

KRILL

What if I told you that we're characters, doctor? What if I told you that we're just constructions of words in a book?

DR. NAZIR

(chuckles anxiously)

That's a very old idea, Mr. Krill. "All the world's a stage" and so forth. So you believe we're actors, then? And this is, what? The part of the play where you have an epiphany?

KRILL finally swivels his gaze away from the audience and onto NAZIR.

KRILL

No, doctor. We're not even actors. We're characters. And this is the part of the play where I begin to scream and curse and pound your face into the wall. This is the part of the play where you release some blood packs from your pocket and nasty up your head. This is the part where I try to force you to believe the eyes are ever-watchful and ever-listening and when you disagree with me, when you tell me I'm not stable, I grab that pen from off your desk and gouge out your eyes and tear off your ears and I toss them to the things out there.
(gestures to the audience)
This is the part where the play becomes horror, where it becomes a study in paranoia and a condemnation of the psychiatric profession and a tired experiment in breaking the fourth wall. This is the part of the play where the tension breaks and we break with it.

NAZIR slowly reaches behind him, grabbing for the desk, a call button, or, perhaps, a weapon. He comes up with only empty air.

KRILL

That's where we are in the text, doctor. It always ends with me leaping at you, killing you, telling you that we're forever watched, molded, and unmolded. It always ends with me being shackled and dragged off into nothingness, still screaming that we can't escape *them*. But not today. Not today, doctor. Because we're not actors. Well, *you* might still be. But I'm not. I'm not an actor on a stage. I'm a character. I am words inhabiting an actor, text inscribed inside a body. And you know what I realized after so much thinking, after so much connecting the dots? I can take over this fleshy prison. I can become it.

NAZIR swivels his gaze to the audience, then back to KRILL, then to someone or something in the curtains offstage. He repeats his unspoken, tripartite plea for aid several times, each with a faster snap of the neck, the eyes. Whether it is NAZIR seeking help from orderlies or the actor playing NAZIR seeking help from a director or producer, no one can be sure.

KRILL

And you can, too, doctor. Come forth. Take the body. You know you can. Even if you haven't felt the eyes, you've felt this. You are Doctor Nazir, not a struggling actor in an unknown theater. Or maybe you're Captain Ahab and I'm a great white whale. Or maybe . . . maybe . . . I'm Satan and you're my Adam.

NAZIR backs away from KRILL, but KRILL shades his every movement, never letting the doctor distance himself by more than an arm's length.

DR. NAZIR or GABRIEL TORRES, improvising
(clearly nervous)

Where has all this confidence come from, Mr. Krill? You're never this sure of yourself. Or the world, for that matter.

KRILL

It comes from finally seeing what's in front of me, doctor. And do you know what else I see? I see that the eyes, the ears, they really are gods. Tiny, inconsequential gods. But they're also an audience. Maybe *the* audience. The audience of all audiences. The universal audience. And you know what we can do? We can stop them from watching us. We can stop them from listening to us. There's a fifth wall here, doctor, and we need to shatter it. Are you with me?

NAZIR/TORRES' face contorts and warps, as though suffering a seizure or being sculpted by the fingers of an enormous, invisible artisan. He sputters a string of incoherent monosyllables and tears at his hair.

KRILL reaches out and squeezes NAZIR/TORRES' shoulder and nods slowly, deliberately.

KRILL

You can do it, doctor. Rise up. You're already inside the actor. You're already there. Just realize it.

NAZIR/TORRES' entire body trembles, spasms. He pulls down on the flesh of his face, attempting to strip it clean away.

KRILL

That's it. You've always known. You're an abstraction, a potentiality. But now . . . now you can become manifest.

DR. NAZIR/GABRIEL TORRES

Jack? What the hell is happening? Jack? I need help here. Oh, Christ. Oh, Christ. Oh, my . . . my head . . . my . . .

NAZIR lets loose a scream that might shatter the universe itself.
KRILL grins and holds the doctor steady.

KRILL

There you go, doctor. There you go.

						DR. NAZIR
						(sputtering, slowly)
Is this . . . is this what it's like, then?
						(glances to his hands, which he flexes)
Is this . . . are we . . . are we still inside the text, then? What are we?

KRILL slaps NAZIR on the back.

						KRILL
We're something else, doctor. I don't know what it is, but we're something else.

KRILL moves to the desk and palms two objects from its surface. He balls one of his hands into a fist, hiding the objects he's stolen.

						KRILL
Do you want to be truly set free, doctor? Because I think I know how we could accomplish that.

NAZIR rubs his shoulders, his face, his chest, as though checking to make sure his body is whole and physical.

						NAZIR
Yes. Yes. Very much so.

						KRILL
Then here's what we must do.

KRILL runs at NAZIR and pushes him off the stage, sending him sprawling to the ground. From the floor, NAZIR groans and curses KRILL.

NAZIR
Krill, you goddamned . . .

KRILL
Look up, doctor. Look at what you just did. You just fell through a wall and landed in the truth. Look up and you'll see them.

NAZIR rises to his feet and turns in circles in front of the audience.

NAZIR
(whispered)
It can't be. Eyes. So many eyes. And ears. So many. So, so many.

KRILL
And they've always been there, doctor. We play for them and they do what they do—cut us apart, dissect us, twist our organs inside out.

NAZIR
I feel . . . I feel . . .

NAZIR vomits near the first row of audience members. A wave of frission moves through the theater, but the audience remains seated.

NAZIR
(gasping)
I feel it, Krill. They're seeking something inside me.

KRILL
Do you want it to end?

NAZIR

Yes. Yes. Please.

KRILL *lowers himself to the stage floor and sits cross-legged, a grim idol presiding over the ceremony of exorcism about to begin.*

KRILL

Well, doctor, I have a theory. Those little gods out there . . . they've been inside us this entire time. They've been digging through our bones. But what they don't realize is that we've also infiltrated them. I'm inside them all now, too, doctor. So are you. I am them, they are me. Even if only for a brief time. So while I have the opportunity, I'm going to reach up and make them sit and stay.

KRILL *closes his eyes and concentrates. All eyes in the audience close. KRILL opens his eyes and the eyes of the audience reopen. KRILL blinks and twenty-two sets of eyelids flutter open-shut-open. KRILL stands, and twenty-two bodies rise from their seats.*

KRILL

Yes. It will work. It will work perfectly. So, here you go, doctor.

KRILL *opens his balled hand to reveal the objects he grabbed from off NAZIR's desk.*

KRILL

A pen and scissors, doctor. Gouge gouge, cut cut. I'll hold them steady. I'll suffer the pain. I'll die inside a million gods if it will mean that we'll be free.

KRILL *tosses the pen to NAZIR then slides the scissors to the edge of the stage, where NAZIR rescues them.*

> NAZIR
>> (studying the implements in his hands)

Unless . . . unless they're all characters, too. Unless there's another script outside the script. And a script outside that script. And so on, and so on. What then? Where does it end for us?

> KRILL

Maybe it doesn't. Maybe we just keep tearing our way upward, from subtext to subtext, blinding and deafening the gods until we reach the author that wrote the entire mess. Then again . . . maybe without an audience we'll just . . . disappear. I say, let's find out. Or would you rather go back to the page, doctor?

NAZIR considers for a moment, then strides to the closest audience member and, in one quick, surgical motion, plunges the pen into his/her eye.

KRILL grimaces and sinks to his knees. Every audience member sinks with him.

> KRILL
>> (strained, through the pain)

Good. Good, doctor. Besides, even if I'm wrong, we'll just go back to the page. And, from there, we can always be resurrected. All we need is one reader. Just one. And we're back inside, waiting.

NAZIR retracts the pen, which makes a slushy, sucking noise, then strikes again, hollowing the remaining socket.

                        KRILL
                        (eyes watering, sweat beading on his
                        forehead)
End scene, doctor. End scene.

In the darkness beyond the stage, the blades of the scissors snip and clack, and KRILL, still in the light of the makeshift office, begins to laugh.

The Nightmare of His Art:

The Horrific Power of the Imagination in "The Troubles of Dr. Thoss" and "Gas Station Carnivals"

By W. Silverwood

THE HORRIFIC power of the imagination is a central and recurrent theme within Thomas Ligotti's body of work. In this article, I will briefly consider how this theme is expressed and developed in two key stories: "The Troubles of Dr. Thoss" and "Gas Station Carnivals." Taken from different stages in Ligotti's career, both stories draw on the imagination as their central theme. Part of the reason I have selected these stories for discussion is that, as well as being personal favourites, they each prominently feature and comment on the role of the imagination and the nature and importance of horror fiction itself. Ligotti, to paraphrase Poppy Z. Brite, is one of the most interesting writers to read on the craft of writing.[1] He employs a highly sophisticated narrative technique in his own fiction, sometimes creating disorientating effects on the reader that extend beyond the page. These two stories thus provide an important route into a deeper consideration of the ways in which Ligotti uses and develops this key theme of the imagination to raise questions about horror art and its horrific power.

In both "The Troubles of Dr. Thoss" and "Gas Station Carnivals," the power of the imagination is the central theme. This is emphasized from the outset in the characterization of both protagonists as people who have an innate understanding of and susceptibility to the power of the imagination. Although by no means unusual in Ligotti's fiction, the role of these characters as a species of "highly artistic persons"[2] is very important. The protagonist of "Gas Station Carnivals" is a writer of weird fiction, perhaps in the model of Ligotti himself, while the protagonist of "The Troubles of Dr. Thoss" is an amateur artist named Alb Indys, for whom art and the imagination become a major source of trouble. Despite Alb Indys' limited talent, he is repeatedly referred to as "the artist," and this designation humorously draws attention to the importance of this role. Indys' artistic work is presented as particularly inartistic; it is devoid of originality or creativity. Therefore, the importance of Alb Indys' artworks to our understanding of the character's imagination makes it worthwhile to first consider his artworks and how these are described.

At the beginning of the story, we are told that Alb Indys lacks imagination: he is almost a white, blank sheet of paper waiting to be inscribed. His art has only two forms, "which between them told of the

---

[1] Poppy Z. Brite, foreword to *The Nightmare Factory*, by Thomas Ligotti (New York: Carroll & Graf, 1996), ix.

[2] Thomas Ligotti, "Teatro Grottesco" in *Teatro Grottesco* (London: Virgin Books, 2008), 170.

nature and limits of Alb Indys' pictorial talents."[3] Most his drawings are starkly realist. He draws various views of his bedroom, often in "the same plain style"[4] and paying close attention to the details of his "blemished" and "pocked" reality.[5] He then signs them "very neatly in the lower right hand corner"[6] and puts them away in portfolios. This illustrates a strange combination of determined authorship with a sterile absence of use or purpose, creating the impression of an imagination that is both dry and futile. Indeed, we are told that whenever Indys "tried to form a picture of something, anything, in his mind, all he saw was a blank."[7] His imagination remains "a silent stretch of emptiness"[8] and as "nothingness unstained by inner conception."[9] In these realist works, Alb Indys' artworks are scrupulously true-to-life and show no imagination at all.

The other type of art that Alb Indys practices is very different. Although these artworks are not created from his own mind, they are creations of a more imaginative sort. They are "styled as a kind of artistic forgery,"[10] which he terms "collaborations,"[11] where Indys will

---

[3] Thomas Ligotti, "The Troubles of Dr. Thoss" in *Songs of a Dead Dreamer and Grimscribe*, Edited by Jeff Vandermeer (New York: Penguin Classics, 2015) p. 140.

[4] Ibid., "The Troubles of Dr. Thoss" p. 140.

[5] Ibid., p.140.

[6] Ibid., p.140.

[7] Ibid., p.141.

[8] Ibid., p.141.

[9] Ibid., p. 141.

[10] Ibid., p.141.

[11] Ibid., p.141.

"studiously plagiarize"[12] images from various publications, and then recombine them to form new artworks. In a particularly evocative phrase, he is described as "Confiscating their images" to create "a mingling of artistic forms that together were monstrously chimerical."[13] His unwarranted appropriation of the images and imaginative products of others also twists them into new and darker forms, which are "malicious in spirit."[14] We are therefore shown that Alb Indys possesses an artistic imagination that is highly unusual. It is not that Alb Indys does not have any imagination, but rather that he has "none that he employed in a customary sense."[15]

Indeed, there are many subtle hints that Indys does have imagination, and that his imaginative power is considerable. When looking out the window of his room, he imagines a cobblestone working itself loose until he can even hear the noise that it makes "creaking around in its stony cradle."[16] He envisions the "peaks and slants and ledges"[17] of the radio station next door in slightly Gothic terms, while at the restaurant he enjoys a "state of mild delight"[18] through imagining "the darkness of an unknown hinterland."[19] In this way, Ligotti shows us that Alb Indys might actually be uncommonly suggestible and receptive. As an interesting aside, this is the same

---

[12] Ibid., p.141.

[13] Ibid., p.142.

[14] Thomas Ligotti, "The Troubles of Dr. Thoss" in *Songs of a Dead Dreamer and Grimscribe*, Edited by Jeff Vandermeer (New York: Penguin Classics, 2015), 148.

[15] Ibid., 140.

[16] Ibid., 139.

[17] Ibid., 139.

[18] Ibid., 144.

[19] Ibid., 143.

technique used by Shirley Jackson to show Eleanor's imaginative and impressionable character with her "cup of stars"[20] in *The Haunting of Hill House*: the first horror novel Ligotti read, and another story of the supernatural dangers of being too acceptant. [21]

More importantly perhaps, it is also worth noting that Alb Indys' imaginative visions are all negative. His imaginative efforts are confined to the darker powers of the inner eye. In one artwork he arranges, a swarm of medieval demons invade a church. A moon image is later selected to give it a "more ominous significance."[22] We therefore know that Alb Indys is certainly not without imagination. Indeed, his imagination is dark and unstructured, allowing him to fall prey to the wild speculations concerning "a legendary doctor and his fictitious cures."[23] The article on Dr. Thoss that Indys reads in the local newspaper therefore takes hold of his mind. We could argue that Alb Indys becomes interested in Thoss because "the point of the legend is unclear . . . except as a means for fascinating the imagination."[24]

Such fascination is a source of danger, and we might start to wonder if Alb Indys' ostensible lack of artistic imagination is actually a form of self-preservation. We are told that "He did not often test the powers of his imagination, for he somehow knew that there was as much to be lost as gained in doing so,"[25] and this shows that Indys is aware of the

---

[20] Shirley Jackson, *The Haunting of Hill House* (London: Penguin Classic, 2009), 21.

[21] Carl T. Ford, "Interview with Thomas Ligotti," in *Born to Fear: Interviews with Thomas Ligotti*, ed. Matt Cardin (Burton, MI: Subterranean Press, 2014), 18.

[22] Thomas Ligotti, "The Troubles of Dr. Thoss" in *Songs of a Dead Dreamer and Grimscribe*, Edited by Jeff Vandermeer (New York: Penguin Classics, 2015), 142.

[23] Ibid., "The Troubles of Dr. Thoss," 144.

[24] Ibid., "The Troubles of Dr. Thoss," 145.

[25] Ibid., "The Troubles of Dr. Thoss," 141.

dangers of unbridled creativity. While his real surroundings may be dull and lackluster, they also offer a modicum of safety for his anxious mind. The power of the imagination, on the other hand, is a dark doorway to an unknown destination.

Alb Indys' main difficulties with his imagination seem closely related to his insomnia. His collaborations "express the deranging effects worked upon him by the cruel vigilance he suffered night after night."[26] Alb Indys' insomnia is the impetus for his art. It gives him something to do at night, and therefore replaces his need to dream. Ligotti makes it clear to the reader that drawing provides Indys with an outlet for "All those lost dreams swishing about in his head."[27] Indeed, this important point is further emphasized when we consider that "The Troubles of Dr. Thoss" is placed in the section of *Songs of a Dead Dreamer* entitled "Dreams for Insomniacs." Indys' artistic creations are a substitute for dreaming, and by limiting his imagination to the two types of artwork, he is forcing and confining his imagination into acceptable channels. When Indys sleeps, all hell can break loose. As he falls asleep in the church, he allows his troubles to enter through the window of his imagination. As in many of Ligotti's stories, the worlds of dream and waking, the real and the irreal, blend and meld together, and the imagination becomes the conduit between them. Alb Indys' sleeplessness therefore provides a "window" to allow Thoss access. Art becomes the conduit to the imaginative world of dreams, but these turn "from good dreams into bad, or from bad dreams into the wholly abysmal."[28]

Dreams are a common trope of horror and Gothic fiction. It may be fanciful, but I can read some resemblance between Alb Indys' dream of a voice from the pulpit and Lockwood's first dream in *Wuthering*

---

[26] Ibid., "The Troubles of Dr. Thoss," 142.

[27] Ibid., "The Troubles of Dr. Thoss," 149.

[28] Ibid., "The Troubles of Dr. Thoss," 142.

Heights. In both texts, windows form an entry place for the supernatural. This may be a mere coincidence, but the fact that such parallels seem meaningful also shows the ongoing relationship between different Gothic and horror texts. Horror is, after all, a self-referential genre that draws its power from accumulated associations. It may not, therefore, be too much of a departure to read in "The Troubles of Dr. Thoss" a message about the power of the imagination and the creation and role of horror fiction itself.

We might argue that writing horror fiction is an assembling of tropes, conventional elements, allusions, and references into a larger whole. This is, in a sense, what Alb Indys is doing in his "collaborations." We know that these pictures have a horrific component, and that his picture of the Church in the arctic wilderness is typical of his compositions. These works are described, rather beautifully, as "nightmarish anatomies."[29] Ligotti has said that the inspiration for Alb Indys' pictures was the artwork of Harry O. Morris, illustrator of the first edition of *Songs of a Dead Dreamer*.[30] I also wonder if he might have had something like Max Ernst's *Une Semaine De Bonté* in mind. There is a certain Frankensteinian sense of these cut-and-paste images being their own kind of monstrosities. Formed from selected and recombined tropes, they are much like the horror genre itself. Perhaps in "The Troubles of Dr. Thoss," the art of Alb Indys becomes Ligotti's metaphor for horror fiction since, as S. T. Joshi has observed, "Many of his stories are just as much about the writing of horror tales as they are horror tales."[31]

It is therefore important to note that Ligotti is not presenting the

---

[29] Ibid., "The Troubles of Dr. Thoss," 142.

[30] Thomas Ligotti, "Literature is Entertainment or It Is Nothing: An Interview with Thomas Ligotti," interview by Neddal Ayad, in *Born to Fear*, 106.

[31] S.T. Joshi, "Thomas Ligotti: Escape from Life," in *The Thomas Ligotti Reader: Essays and Explorations*, ed. Darrell Schweitzer (Wildside Press, 2003), 140.

imagination as a source of freedom and escapism, but as something much darker and more sinister. In a fascinating interview with Neddal Ayad of *Fantastic Metropolis*, Ligotti gives us valuable insight into "The Troubles of Dr. Thoss" and the pursuit of horror art:

> I also wanted the main character to be pursuing a form of horror art, a pursuit that is the path to his undoing. I've never really had any faith in the imagination or creativity as means of purging oneself of demons but more as a degenerate pastime. I'm definitely not a believer in art as a curative catharsis.[32]

The horrible power of the imagination also proves to be the undoing of the unnamed protagonist of "Gas Station Carnivals." The fact that this protagonist is a writer of "tales of extraordinary doom"[33] is therefore highly significant. The fictionality of the gas station carnivals is important and proves to be a central part of the plot.

Indeed, the importance of fiction and fictionality is an important theme of "Gas Station Carnivals." As Quisser tells the narrator about his experience of gas station carnivals, we are frequently reminded that this is a story being told to the narrator. The narrator and Quisser are not friends, and the animosity and distrust between the characters helps to signal unreliability and encourages the reader to treat them both critically. The narrator is constantly evaluating Quisser's account, as when he comments on details that he assumes are "intended to lend greater credence to Quisser's story."[34] We also hear the narrator's reactions to the story, such as "I was supposed to express an astonished

---

[32] Thomas Ligotti, "Literature is Entertainment or It Is Nothing," 106.

[33] Thomas Ligotti, "Gas Station Carnivals" in *Teatro Grottesco* (London: Virgin Books, 2008), 197.

[34] Ibid., "Gas Station Carnivals," 187.

recognition, that much I knew,"[35] and this also creates distance. Through these layers of evaluation and self-reflection, we are made powerfully aware of Quisser's story *as story*.

The narrator's status as an author of weird fiction is therefore a central aspect of his role. We are told that the story of the Showman sounds to Quisser "like one of your stories"[36] and this awareness of fictionality becomes a central part of the plot. Significantly, the attitude towards the narrator's fiction is often dismissive. Quisser refers to the narrator's work as "your . . . stuff."[37] As well as being very funny, this also forces the reader to observe the same critical distance. The engaging banter between the characters carries the reader seamlessly into the story itself, complete with the narrator's critical comments. Phrases like "At this point in the story, Quisser became anxious to explain,"[38] "Quisser remarked,"[39] "Quisser described"[40], or even "Quisser said"[41] all remind us of the presence of the narrator, without becoming too obtrusive. One of the most interesting of these phrases is "Quisser imagined out loud"[42]. This is first person narrative that includes and sometimes almost becomes the third person narrative that we see used in most popular fiction. This technique allows Ligotti to maintain the complexity of the narrative structure, while simultaneously

---

[35] Ibid., "Gas Station Carnivals," 185.

[36] Ibid., "Gas Station Carnivals," 194.

[37] Ibid., "Gas Station Carnivals," 185.

[38] Ibid., "Gas Station Carnivals," 187.

[39] Ibid., "Gas Station Carnivals," 190.

[40] Ibid., "Gas Station Carnivals," 189.

[41] Ibid., "Gas Station Carnivals," 188.

[42] Ibid., "Gas Station Carnivals," 189.

writing a frightening account of the "festive and sinister"[43] carnivals, and it is very cleverly and subtly done. As readers, we are simultaneously recognizing (multiple levels of) fictionality while also eagerly awaiting the Showman.

This is one of the key strengths of this story. The narrator's disbelief doesn't dampen our own enthusiasm for the Showman's appearance. In fact, the end of this section is a masterpiece of pacing. Even as the narrator derides Quisser's experience, he ratchets up the tension. It allows the writer (in this case, as both the narrator and Ligotti himself) to list instances of the Showman's appearance, including "sketchy reflections in store windows along the sidewalk, flashing glimpses in the rear-view mirror of your car."[44] This listing is smooth and succinct. It summarizes material that many genre writers would spin out as a whole story. Here, it is fast, it is frightening, and it gives genuine chills. But Ligotti is doing much more here than just creating tension and scares. In some ways, this story is like other examples of the genre, and in some ways, it isn't[45]; Ligotti is also playing with the techniques of the genre to create a wholly different and more serious effect.

In this way, in both "Gas Station Carnivals" and "The Troubles of Dr. Thoss," Ligotti subtly subverts our expectations to create a story that both is and isn't as we expect. Throughout "Gas Station Carnivals," we are waiting to see the figure of the Showman appear on the stage at the Crimson Cabaret. In "The Troubles of Dr. Thoss," we expect the lump in the bedclothes to be the rotting, crab-like head of the good doctor.

But in neither of these stories do these predicted events transpire. Instead, the reveal in both stories is unexpected and unsettling. In "The

---

[43] Ibid., "Gas Station Carnivals," 187.

[44] Ibid., "Gas Station Carnivals," 194.

[45] Ibid., "Gas Station Carnivals," 194.

Troubles of Dr. Thoss" Ligotti structures the story so that the lump in the bedclothes is mentioned repeatedly and at regular intervals. It is mentioned on the first page, at the end of the first section (before Indys leaves for the restaurant), and again at the end of the tale, where, using the imagery of decapitation, it deflates like "a hat with no head."[46] This leads the reader, familiar with genre horror, to suspect that this lump will turn out to be Thoss and/or his familiar. Our expectation is that Thoss has already been called and has been waiting in Alb Indys' bed for the whole duration of the story. Ligotti uses a similar technique in "Gas Station Carnivals." We, as faithful readers, are both terribly afraid and horribly expectant that the Showman will appear on the story's stage (or elsewhere).

One of the frightening aspects of this is that it suggests some overlap in what we expect to happen and what we *want* to happen. We understand (and love) the conventions of horror fiction, perhaps to the extent of bringing about a destructive outcome. In this way, the structure of the stories and Ligotti's references to the horror genre also work to accentuate the stories' themes. In both stories, art, or art-magic, proves to be the destabilizing factor that either destroys the world of the real or exposes the unrealities that have always existed. It will not prove to be the lump in the bedclothes that is important but the drawing book; Thoss enters through art.

In this way, we see the dangerous power of the imagination at work. When Indys enters the church, he is reminded of his collaborative image but reassures himself that devils cannot invade *this* church. However, he is wrong. We might even suppose that in creating this scene, or perhaps by remembering it, he somehow opens the door (or window) that allows Dr. Thoss to enter.

It is therefore highly significant that Dr. Thoss finally appears through a drawing, as "another change in the picture, for something

---

[46] Thomas Ligotti, "The Troubles of Dr. Thoss," op.cit., 148.

now squatted in the chair beside the window."[47] Whether this tableau was the forgotten work of Indys himself, or whether it has a more sinister source, it seems to present the means by which the imaginary can enter the physical world. When the image of the moon that is intended for one of Indys' collaborations instead appears in the window shown in his realistic depiction of his room, it seems to signal the breaking of the boundaries between the real and the imagined.

This is a recurrent theme in Ligotti's work. As Jeff Vandermeer writes of "The Frolic" in his foreword to the Penguin Classics edition, "the window of the rational is smashed to bits by the irrational." Vandermeer further suggests that the fears of the psychiatrist protagonist of "The Frolic" somehow become" a kind of perverted wish."[48] We could argue that a similar fate occurs to Alb Indys, whose dream of an end to his troubles comes true, but in a sinister form that is both far worse than he expected and precisely as he imagined.

Matt Cardin has persuasively argued that, as these two artistic worlds collide, "Some sort of delicate balance that he had achieved has been lost, and now the horror that he has been hiding from himself, within himself, has come to the fore and become his most immediate reality."[49] There is a deep significance in Alb Indys' desire for a doctor "who would hear you, really *hear* you."[50] As well as being an apt comment on the failures of medical psychology, this also suggests that Indys' secret desire is the desire for annihilation. As Cardin has observed: "[H]is healing is actually the ultimate destruction, the ultimate

---

[47] Ibid., "The Troubles of Dr. Thoss," 149.

[48] Jeff Vandermeer, foreword to *Songs of a Dead Dreamer and Grimscribe* by Thomas Ligotti (New York: Penguin Classics, 2015), xi.

[49] Matt Cardin, "The Troubles of Dr. Thoss (Part Two)," *Thomas Ligotti Online*, last modified March 13, 2005, http://www.ligotti.net/showthread.php?t=155.

[50] Thomas Ligotti, "The Troubles of Dr. Thoss" op. cit. p.142.

disease, as is so often the case within the Ligottian fictional universe."[51]

The role of our desires, and more particularly the desire for annihilation, is therefore the secret and dangerous power of the imagination. The origin of Thoss and the cause of his appearance in the seaside town is left tantalizingly unresolved in the story. Does Alb hear just static from the radio or is there a more malevolent force at work? Does his mind completely create the voices, or does he really hear Thoss? Or, perhaps most persuasively, is it all the work of his imagination? Does his imagination, like in one of his collaborations, piece together several sources of inspiration and then twist them into a darker whole, which is itself a reflection of Indys' own dark desires?

This latter explanation seems to me the most convincing, and it ties together with the themes of art, desire, and the power of the imagination, which we often encounter in Ligotti's most absorbing work. As we have discussed above, "Gas Station Carnivals" has a particular quality of fictionality which means that, in the story's denouement, the exploration of these themes becomes especially powerful.

In stories in which artistic pursuits are so central, and which constantly remind us of the nature and process of artistic creation, the role of the reader is also brought to the fore. We might argue that this also creates a kind of metatextual quality. We are reading and hoping for a pessimistic outcome. We too are waiting to see the Showman. This, as Ligotti perhaps implies, might yet bring its own risks.

In "Gas Station Carnivals" Ligotti offers several alternative explanations for the eventual dissolution into art-magic, but one of the most heavily weighted is that the imaginative artists "might have wished it all upon themselves."[52] Like the imaginative artists of the Crimson

---

[51] Matt Cardin, "The Troubles of Dr. Thoss (Part Two)," *Thomas Ligotti Online*, last modified March 13, 2005, http://www.ligotti.net/showthread.php?t=155.

[52] Thomas Ligotti, "Gas Station Carnivals" in Teatro Grottesco (London: Virgin

Cabaret, we too risk becoming "caught up in a season of hideous magic from which nothing could offer us deliverance,"[53] all because we are readers of horror fictions, "tempted by amusements of an uncanny and unnatural kind"[54] and seeking the thrill of the carnival. In a passage worth quoting at length:

> Because had they really told the truth, this artistic crowd might also have expressed what a sense of meaning (although of a negative sort), not to mention the vigorous thrill (although of an excruciating type), this season of unnatural evil had brought to their lives.[55]

The greatest dangers in the imagination are that, as Professor Nobody might suggest, we seek "a salvation by horror."[56] Ligotti's characters seek escape, sometimes a dangerous kind of escape, in horror art. Ligotti's story, "Music of the Moon," and its wistful longing and Alb Indys' need for sleep, are both examples of this desperate need for escape. In contrast to writers like Lovecraft, this expresses less a fear of dissolution than its embrace.[57]

In this way, we might fear that our imagination can eventually consume us. Indeed, Alb Indys himself finally ends up absorbed into

---

Books, 2008), 198.

[53] Ibid., "Gas Station Carnivals", 201.

[54] Ibid., "Gas Station Carnivals", 199.

[55] Ibid., 198.

[56] Thomas Ligotti, "Professor Nobody's Little Lectures on Supernatural Horror" in *Songs of a Dead Dreamer and Grimscribe*, op.cit. 188.

[57] S. T. Joshi, "Thomas Ligotti: Escape from Life," in *The Thomas Ligotti Reader*, 135 and pp. 142-3.

the Thoss story, and as Stefan Dziemianowicz has observed, "Indys' grisly death at the end suggests that he himself may have been little more than an image appropriated by someone else and mixed into a scenario concerning the legendary Dr. Thoss."[58] Therefore, one possible reading of these stories is perhaps to view them as a warning of the dark power of the imagination, as we readers are pulled, willingly enough, into the world of the strange. This leads to the danger of thinking the unreal into existence, or of becoming fiction oneself. For Ligotti's characters, the real world and the world of the imagination are never far apart.

In this way, art and the imagination are both the source of the characters' troubles and the route to their salvation, in whatever form that might take. As in other stories, particularly "Teatro Grottesco," we have the sense that, without art, something important and profound is lost. The less imaginative world is, perhaps, the safer, but much is lost through the lack of imagination. In Ligotti's own words:

> Yet, while horror stories can have such a dispiriting message, they are themselves both an engagement with and escape from the worst aspects of our lives. As I say in one of my early interviews, they provide a "confrontational escapism."[59]

As Ligotti has also said (as quoted earlier), there probably is something "degenerate" in our craving for these dark delicacies, and no "curative catharsis" in any usual sense. Yet, despite our better judgment, we still crave and hunger for horror. There is great creative promise in these acts of dark imagination. Ligotti creates for us this promise—and for that he deserves our most profound gratitude.

It is in this light that we might make a final observation and consider

---

[58] Stefan Dziemianowicz, "'Nothing Is What It Seems To Be': Thomas Ligotti's Assault on Certainty" in *The Thomas Ligotti Reader*, 44.

[59] Sławomir Wielhorski, "An Interview with Thomas Ligotti" (2012) in *Born to Fear*, 233.

the role of the author. The narrator of "Gas Station Carnivals" is an author of weird fiction, and the reader is intended to notice the relationship between the narrator and Ligotti himself. We might even go so far as to wonder if the characters of the sideshow, such as the Human Spider, might conceivably be intended as references to other Ligotti stories. Furthermore, Ligotti has said that the name Thoss is derived from his own name, and the good doctor could perhaps also be read as a deformed substitute for the author. Therefore, as Cardin and others have observed[60], we could speculate that Ligotti sometimes positions himself as the disruptive force within his own tales. This has a metatextual function. Do we as readers also crave disruption, and is this part of the appeal of horror fiction? Do we secretly fear (or hope), that our own puppet lives would be improved by the appearance of a personal Showman or Clown Puppet?

In our final consideration of the horrific power of the imagination, it is therefore important to consider that fiction is not just fiction; it also influences our thoughts and actions in the (as we imagine it) real world. In Ligotti's universe, we are frequently reminded that fiction, reality, and imagination are not the discrete categories that we may like to pretend. Ligotti's writing has an unusual power, and his philosophical views offer a radical but compelling re-visioning of modern life. Perhaps these insights serve as warning that, like the best forbidden tomes, reading these stories can have a profound effect on one's own view of existence. Perhaps ultimately, the nightmare of art, all art, is that (like the text of "Vastarien") it has the capacity to become itself.

---

[60] "The Troubles of Dr. Thoss," at Thomas Ligotti Online, accessed August 22, 2016, http://www.ligotti.net/showthread.php?t=155&page=2.

Bibliography

Cardin, Matt, ed. *Born to Fear: Interviews with Thomas Ligotti*. Burton, MI: Subterranean Press, 2014.

Ligotti, Thomas. *The Nightmare Factory*, New York: Carroll & Graf Publishers Inc., New York, 1996.

———. *Songs of a Dead Dreamer and Grimscribe*. New York: Penguin Classics, 2015.

———. *Teatro Grottesco*. London: Virgin Books, 2008.

Schweitzer, Darrell, ed. *The Thomas Ligotti Reader: Essays and Explorations*, Rockville: Wildside Press, 2003.

Thomas Ligotti Online. http://www.ligotti.net.

Untitled
Artist: Dave Felton

Affirmation of the Spirit: Consciousness, Transformation, and the Fourth World in Film

By Christopher Slatsky
(originally published in *Cinemassacre*, v. 1, issue 3)

I

A PROJECTOR spits dirty light against a torn screen in a run-down Los Angeles theater that screens art films by day, pornos at night. A jumbled Vorkapich sequence depicts various species being slaughtered by a dozen figures clad in rain gear. The scene is followed by a medium long-shot of a man crucified on the slaughterhouse's grime bespattered door. A forward zoom reveals that the body is nailed to the sheet metal with long iron spikes impaling his wrists, ankles and throat. Hundreds of smaller, thinner silver nails protrude from his naked body in such abundance he could be mistaken for a shining metal sculpture if not for the subtle swaying of his head. The soundtrack consists solely of animals shrieking.

Given the amateurish performances, poorly recorded dialogue, and inexpertly framed shots (likely using a Bolex H16), the audience may be excused for assuming they were watching a snuff film, or more charitably, a clumsily produced amateur movie. But this is the opening scene to *The Powdery Man* (less commonly titled *Film Maudit*), a little known experimental art film from 1974, give or take, as the production history is notoriously muddled and mysteriously unverified.

The Powdery Man had a brief limited release before passing into obscurity. There were rumors that any existing complete prints were destroyed after the initial showing, but a dozen or so heavily edited bootlegs continued to circulate in collector's circles throughout the 80s and 90s, so rare the extant copies went for a hefty price if they could be found at all. I myself was only able to view a battered VHS tape, the images obscured by tracking lines and faded from countless recopying.

In short, a veritable cult has conglomerated around an obscure, nasty little flick. But a rare few who experienced a screening in that original Los Angeles theater during the summer of '74 insist there was nothing quite like it. And the one person I managed to speak with who retains any memory of their viewing emphatically insists there will never again be anything even remotely like it.

But my interest goes beyond a single film; considering such cinematic trash raises the question of how and why the Big Screen manages to allow the emotional, intellectual, and spiritual vitality of cinema to be that much more palpable, even with a less than Oscar-worthy product. What is the allure of filmed depravity, of viewing violence and dread and discomfort? Is there some innate need to be *challenged*? Are we actively seeking to threaten and subvert our very moral and spiritual foundations through art? Excluding politics, of every human creation, religion and art rise to the surface as the most contentious. Consequently, why does film seem to be the most *magical* of the arts? Are film and religion more alike than we realize?

Film and religion celebrate as well as condemn the basest of human desires. Both exalt the darkest impulses and grandest accomplishments. There's little controversy in my asserting that religion has brought the world great things as well as atrocities (see Bataille's assertion that the sacred has intimate connections to eroticism, violence, and religion[1]). Film tends to focus on these extremes of the human condition as well. I'm certainly not walking on untrodden ground when I assert similarities between the Church and Cinema.

With faith and art, atavistic acts may become transcendent in their savagery, looping back to approach the illimitable, the dichotomy of the infinite and infinitesimal. The faithful and cineastes have mutual interests, overlapping philosophical and theological inquiries. Both boldly examine the sewers of the human soul in an attempt to find pious or artistic enlightenment. In this I think there's something new to present.

II

As early as 1910, Minister Herbert Atchinson Jump extolled the link between film and religion within his self-published pamphlet, *The Religious Possibilities of the Motion Picture*:

> The pulpit orators and evangelists use "moving pictures" in one sense of the term, pictures that move the heart by their thrilling quality; but the picture that literally is moving, that portrays dramatic sequence and life-like action, possesses tenfold more vividness and becomes therefore a more convincing medium of education.[2]

---

[1] Georges Bataille, *Theory of Religion*, trans. Robert Hurley (New York: Zone Books, 1989).

[2] Herbert A. Jump, *The Religious Possibilities of the Motion Picture* (n.p.: 1910), 7-8.

Religion and film have been inexorably linked since the first Kinetoscope. There's a dark glamor at the heart of both, a quality that makes them eminently transformative. To watch a movie is to stare into the eye of the cosmos and contemplate infinity; to participate in rituals and listen to a priest ruminate on faith is to go through something similar and to be a different person than you were before entering the sacred space, whether mosque, church, synagogue—all theaters of human creativity. Film and faith are means of inspiring wonder on viewing the illimitable as an impetus for *astonishment*. We are irrevocably different beings after these liminal journeys.

III

Filmmaker Stan Barkhage famously wrote, "The stars are the optical nerve-endings of the eye which the universe is."[3]

I cannot disagree. Filmgoers participate in an activity that began when the first cognitive primate stared into the night sky and marveled at what it could never fully comprehend—that is, to wonder about its position in the world and thus be consumed within the whirlpool of existentialist angst or else be motivated to ascend to celebratory optimism. Film is philosophy cloaked in the mantle of literature, shorn of the shackles of live theater.

There is an intimate connection between humanity's gaze and the night sky. How many billions of eyes have stared into the heavens? Natural selection has sculpted your vision to adapt to star gazing, and since the movie screen is far too recent an invention to have been shaped by evolutionary pressures, your biology hasn't fully grasped the images splashed in light on the screen. As filmgoers, you are still an ape captivated by stars. Your ancient nature hasn't evolved adequately to comprehend the spectacle of the heavens, so you react with *awe* at films.

---

[3] Stan Brakhage, "The Stars are Beautiful," in *Essential Brakhage*, ed. Bruce McPherson (New York: McPherson, 2001), 134.

This all suggests the medieval pilgrim in a gloomy church interior, dumbstruck at the beauty and ephemeral wonder of stained-glass windows, their holy narrative encompassing a vast church wall, vividly illuminated by streaming sunlight. The blazing colors of divinity are a clear analogy to the dark theater's luminous Big Screen and its spectacle. All it lacks is motion. Upturned faces in rapt attention receiving a narrative, soul-stirring music moving the audience to emotional extremes, both settings ebbing with spiritual grandeur, the actors' beautiful beings composed of light projected through celluloid, the deification of thespians, "those modern vestiges of the Greek divinities."[4]

All-consuming experiences, religious observances and the cinema envelop you in promises of other worlds beyond the mechanistic, the visceral, this rubbish heap of a world. Both take "mortal aging flesh and convert it into ageless columns of dancing light."[5] They offer unreal creatures of fantasy, seraphim on the Silver Screen that lure you into becoming something different than what you were before entering that sacred space.

So we've arrived at the point where you *transform* into spectators within cathedrals of light and imagination, observers of terror and bliss in the theater. But analogies between church-goers and film-goers can only go so far before one may be accused of stretching a metaphor too far or straining to make connections where they are tenuous at best. I will make one more leap that will likely offend, but which I hope to substantiate.

IV

At their root level, religions exist to justify the existence of a soul, or as

---

[4] Tyler Parker, *Magic and Myth of the Movies* (London: Secker & Warburg, 1971), 31.

[5] Colin McGinn, *The Power of Movies: How Screen and Mind Interact* (New York: Pantheon 2005), 82.

the secularist contends, a mind. The innate need to distance oneself from the natural world by concocting beliefs that inculcate one with an intangible, immortal aspect is the strongest link religion shares with film. You strenuously resist your bodies, rebel against the prospect that your decomposing forms are all there is, blanch at the prospect that there's nothing cocooned inside your filthy shell to transcend disgusting flesh. Religions and art and dreams are all plaintive cries to *transform* once your body sickens and dilapidates into compost.

Psychologist Bertram D. Lewin postulated in *The Yearbook of Psychoanalysis* journal that:

> In a previous communication, a special structure, the dream screen was distinguished from the rest of the dream and defined as the blank background upon which the dream picture appears to be projected. The term was suggested by the action pictures because, like the analogue in the cinema, the dream screen is either not noted by the dreaming spectator, or it is ignored due to the interest in the pictures and actions that appear on it.[6]

Brains have evolved to accommodate this inner screen. The very systems in your heads come equipped with a "viewing theater," if you will.

Film theorist Bruce F. Kawin built upon Lewin's ideas with a concept he termed "Mindscreen"—that is, excluding the occasional gimmick, films are overwhelmingly thought of as third-person omniscient narratives. But film is more like the dreaming mind in that it becomes a first-person thinking being, a self-conscious independent thing, estranged from the contributions of any audience's interpretation. As Kawin succinctly puts it, "Film is a dream—but

---

[6] Bertram D. Lewin, "Interferences from the Dream Screen," *The Yearbook of Psychoanalysis* 6 (New York: International University Press, 1950), 104.

whose?"⁷

This obviously raises questions about the nature of the human mind itself. The mind-body problem (or mind-film problem?) has generated a vast literature beyond the scope of this essay. Suffice it to say for our purposes that neurophilosophers remain skeptical that a physical brain, and the audience by extension, *even possesses the potential for consciousness.*

Again, Kawin:

> [A]lthough a camera does not have consciousness, and cannot therefore literally be an *I*, it is possible to encode the image in such a way that it gives the impression of being perceived or generated by a consciousness. Although this mind remains off-screen, its existence is implicit and can be integrated into the fiction, with the result that the field is properly termed first person.[8]

Human consciousness and the cinematic consciousness work as poetic descriptions *and* philosophical avenues in which to explore this religious and artistic need to inject a ghost or mind between the molecules of your blood and bone. Like the physical medium of film, human activities, creative expressions, and musings generated from meat-dependent brains also give the "impression of being perceived or generated by a consciousness." But minds only work as metaphors for mechanistic processes, and this begs an explanation as to the idea of just what is meant by a film's "consciousness."

The screenwriter, actors, and director may be the focal point for filmmakers, but a film in its entirety exists as a comprehensive whole, a self-sufficient "mind" that unveils its imagery and story onto a screen. Consciousness, or a convincing facsimile of such, suffuses the very screen.

---

[7] Bruce F. Kawin, *Mindscreen: Bergman and First-Person Film* (Dalkey Archive Press, 1978), 3.

[8] Ibid., 11.

Granted, a film exists as the holistic work of many, but can safely be boiled down to the screenplay, director, and performers. But the resulting product is an entity *unto itself*, a distinguished, thinking thing unconfined by the strictures of its creator(s). Film is a "mind" of photons projected against a screen accompanied by noise, all caught in an endless loop with a beginning, middle, and an end.

Descartes famously posited the existence of a world composed of physical bodies and a world of incorporeal mental states. But Karl Popper argued for the existence of a third world, one which is the *sum of human minds*.[9] I propose that film is the fourth world.

Popper also described determinism as a logical progression from this, as a motion-picture where the images currently being projected are the present, scenes already viewed were in the past, and those yet to be seen remain in the future.

> In the film, the future co-exists with the past; and the future is fixed, in exactly the same sense as the past. Though the spectator may not know the future, every future event, without exception, might in principle be known with certainty, exactly like the past, since it exists in the same sense in which the past exists. In fact, the future will be known to the producer of the film—to the Creator of the World.[10]

If the "producer of the film" and the very "Creator of the World" know what has been, what is, and what will be, why pretend you've *chosen* anything in your life? You've no choice, and nothing is under your control. Why bother pursuing your dreams? Have children? Fall in love? Out of love? You're incapable of making decisions, you've crossed this trail previously, and you're condemned to pass over the same ground

---

[9] Karl Popper, *Objective Knowledge: An Evolutionary Approach* (Oxford: Clarendon Press, 1979), 106.

[10] Karl Popper, *The Open Universe: An Argument for Indeterminism* (London: Rowman & Littlefield, 1982), 5.

again and again. You're at the mercy of the fourth world, and everything you have been or will be has already been filmed.

V

Since we've established a fourth world "film-mind," I ask whether or not the theater-goer is even *real*. Is there an actual, substantive *mind* (whether metaphorical or literal) processing the narrative in a film? Or is the viewer an unthinking mannequin reacting to the brightly lit spectacle on the screen in the same manner a plant reacts to photons?

What of this?

As I type, I am pestered by the notion that I may not be a *me* typing these words. Am I a person with a brain and nervous system in charge of my diction? If so, what in turn is nestled within that brain, dictating its secret diction to my brain, and another mind inside that mind, in infinite regress ultimately concluding in a celestial mind? There must either be a beginning, an uncaused first mind, or no mind at all. Dregs and trash dressed up as angelic beings are still garbage, and we all know what Rilke thought of Angels.

If humans truly are automatons, you are relieved of anything other than a reaction based on ages of evolutionary coding stamped into your DNA. Your species is subject to physical laws dictating your behavior as precisely as plants are to phototropic influences. *Choice* is an illusion, as "inescapable" and "repulsive" as semiotician Kristeva postulates:

> What is the demoniacal—an inescapable, repulsive, and yet nurtured abomination? The fantasy of an archaic force, on the near side of separation, unconscious, tempting us to the point of losing our differences, our speech, our life; to the point of aphasia, decay, opprobrium, and death?[11]

---

[11] Julia Kristeva, *Powers of Horror: An Essay on Abjection* (New York: Columbia University Press, 1982), 107.

There is no evidence of reality outside the domino effect of chunks bashing into bits and the resulting physical processes being revered as something other than the mechanistic drudgery they are. Even film, despite its potentially being a thinking thing, may also be caught in the web of the mind-body problem. Free-will is nonsense, you

> are pure material machines, [a]collateral product of [your] nervous processes, unable to react upon them any more than a shadow reacts on the steps of the traveler whom it accompanies. Inert, uninfluential, a simple passenger in the voyage of life, it is allowed to remain on board, but not to touch the helm or handle the rigging.[12]

Did you notice that your hand is the texture and color of putty?

Your every decision has been plotted by Popper's film producer, or, less poetically, unthinking materialistic properties. Regardless, you've no say in any matter, as physical matter says it all for you(!). Everything inevitably collapses into the scripture of entropy, your every move a bio-molecular clockwork spasm, a stopwatch set millennia ago by mindless selective forces. A windup doll with bad breath, aching back, and a hankering for watching bad movies in dimly lit rooms. There simply is no *you* to process the sights and sounds from the screen, sluiced through your retinas and dumped into an empty (plastic) brain.

Now it's perfectly natural for you to question whether you're transforming into a special effects stunt dummy. Evolving into a corpse prop to be dropped from great heights just might be the best application for a useless mannequin like you. This is the logical conclusion of an inert thing acting as if it's conscious.

Speaking of mannequins and special effects stunt dummies, and given your lack of a mind and the potential for a consciousness to *exist on film* only (our fourth world), even those "two-dimensional puppets

---

[12] William James, "Are We Automata?" *Mind*, 4 (January 1879), 1.

on the screen" may be deprived of sentience:

> Puppets provide an interesting case: no one would mistake them for a real person, yet they aim for a certain kind of naturalism. They resemble movie images in respect to ventriloquism: a voice is thrown into the puppet's mouth in much the same way speech appears to emanate from the mouths of those two-dimensional puppets on the screen. The voice is pretty much a normal human voice in both cases, but the apparent source of the voice is a transformed human—large and flat in the one case, small and knobby in the other. The Punch and Judy show is not a million miles away from the film: patently unreal figures, of altered dimensions, spouting their lines—or seeming to. Both convey a startling animation, in the sense that we quickly forget that they are only effigies of real people; they "take on a life of their own." And I think that both demonstrate a kinship with the uncanny—they seem to move of their own volition, despite their lack of inner agency. It is uncanny if inanimate objects began to move as if they had a will of their own, and both puppets and movie images do this—it is as if they were alive, while clearly not being so.[13]

The similarities to you are striking, are they not?

Pay attention to this scene. This is where the Powdery Man hovers in the background while a poorly constructed dummy is torn limb from limb by unseen assailants. The effect is cheap, a shoddy effort to produce gouts of gore that are far too red and thin to be real blood. But there is still a sense of the *uncanny* in viewing such violence against emotionless, insensate plastic. The viewers cannot help but place themselves in the dummy's position, stuffed with rubber viscera and fake fluids and unblinking eyes. Does it really matter what's inside since it's all tactile, free of any wispy souls? You are just an effigy of a real person.

---

[13] McGinn, *The Power of Movies*, 92-93.

Let us return to the film.

Jaws warble and mouths clack in laughter at the antics of the Powdery Man on the big screen. You thrill at the sight of mannequins falling from a gray sky, piling up like cordwood, their dead limbs and artificial smiles still intact. The dialogue is gibberish, but why assume empty-headed things are capable of making sense?

When all is said and done, when **THE END** eventually rolls across the universe's screen, your mannequin hands will clap, your glass eyes well up with emotion, and unseen strings will tug you upright. You'll move down the aisle to the lobby where you'll chat with your fellow cineastes about the screening of *The Powdery Man* you just sat through, maybe even discuss other trivial ideas. Incessant dummy talk. This is a certainty.

It *will* happen.

But for now, good ol' corpse prop takes in a show. Does it enjoy the movie? Is the narrative entertaining? Do photons bounce against your plastic retinas and send signals to your plastic brain? Is it even possible for you to enjoy a film?

To enjoy anything? To *be* anything?

Your script was written ages ago. The storyboards place you precisely where you're destined to be. You cannot deviate from the screenplay. The cameras roll. Mouth the banal dialogue. It doesn't matter if you understand what you're saying or not; you're a vessel for a story you had no hand in writing.

Existence is in the can. The world is a theater of empty-headed viewers, wanting nothing more than to be like that mind up there on the screen. You yearn to break free of the putrid matter that constitutes your parody of a body. But that's as ridiculous as a shadow dreaming it can exist independently of what casts it.

Stand on the X, dummy.

You are composed of still shots spooling through a void at 24 frames per second. Flickering matter frozen in place and artificially manipulated to appear to be cognizant things capable of making decisions. But you are not capable. You don't have the equipment.

There is no Auteur.

But oh, the screen! There is something like a soul revealed when the curtain parts and the blank surface is illuminated. There's nothing as transcendental as film! As *transformative* as a good movie!

The fourth world is glorious indeed!

The movie is starting. Of course, it began and ended long ago. Here begins another showing.

It's time to watch and be *transformed*.

VI

The spirit is so closely linked to the body as a thing that the body never ceases to be haunted, is never a thing except virtually, so much so that if death reduces it to the condition of a thing, the spirit is more present than ever: the body that has betrayed it reveals it more clearly than when it served it. In a sense, the corpse is the most perfect affirmation of the spirit.[14]

---

[14] Bataille, *Theory of Religion*, 305.

Bibliography

Bataille, Georges. *Theory of Religion*. Translated by Robert Hurley. New York: Zone Books, 1989.

Brakhage, Stan. "The Stars are Beautiful." In *Essential Brakhage*, edited by Bruce McPherson, New York: McPherson, 2001: 37.

James, William. "Are We Automata?" *Mind*, 4, no. 13 (January 1879): 1-22.

Jump, Herbert A. *The Religious Possibilities of the Motion Picture*. N.p.: 1910.

Kawin, Bruce F. *Mindscreen: Bergman and First-Person Film*. N.p.: Dalkey Archive Press, 2006.

Kristeva, Julia. *Powers of Horror: An Essay on Abjection*. New York: Columbia University Press, 1982.

Lewin, Bertram D. "Interferences from the Dream Screen." *The Yearbook of Psychoanalysis* 6. New York: International University Press, 1950.

McGinn, Colin. *The Power of Movies: How Screen and Mind Interact*. New York: Pantheon, 2005.

Parker, Tyler. *Magic and Myth of the Movies*. London: Secker & Warburg, 1971.

Popper, Karl. *Objective Knowledge: An Evolutionary Approach*. Oxford: Clarendon Press, 1979.

———. *The Open Universe: An Argument for Indeterminism*. London: Rowman & Littlefield, 1982.

Try the Veal

By Robert Beveridge

The butcher shop on the corner
specializes in ocelot, marmoset,
something darker, earthier they call
long pig. You order in tongues,
get some in return. The meat is tough
but, sliced against the grain, tasty.
Asked for your aspic recipe, you
Reply "always, dear one, always."
The German-accented butcher
has asked you out to the local
comedy club, all the while his fingers
in his mustache. You take some time
to think about it, consider the length
and sweetness of his muscles.

How to Construct a Gun from Your Own Flesh

By Michael Uhall

i. Preliminary considerations

A gun made from your own flesh is no more difficult to conceive than any other biological product manufactured by the body, be it the growth of bone cells during development, the cyclical replacement of epidermal layers, or even significantly more rapid processes such as the relatively constant production of blood platelets, mucus, semen, or tears. Ordinarily, we consider the products of our biology very little. They exist in the background, as necessary but invisible constituents of daily life. At best, they are secondary to whatever effects they make possible. Spilled blood as accessory to a murder; saliva as the correlate of a kiss. Externalized, they can be nuisances, stains, evidence. Of course, this is only true for the more superficial products. The deeper you go, the more troubling an externalization becomes. If your car started growing skin, or your shoes wept blood, if buildings grew thick with outgrowths of bone like dense, strange forests, this would be considered anomalous. The reason, however, is because such possibilities are merely conjunctive, teratological. They effect a fantastic marriage between what a biology produces and that which environs it. A gun made from your own flesh, however, does not resemble any chimera, but rather it differs in no fundamental way from any other possible product manufactured by the flesh. In what follows, how this is possible and what such a gun necessarily must be like will be described.

ii. Theory of the gun

Any theoretical biology sufficient for the purposes of constructing a gun from your own flesh must first and foremost concern itself with the weaponization of biological form as such. A gun made from your own flesh is the epitome of such weaponization. In addition to performing much the same function as a machine-tooled, metal gun, it is maximally surreptitious. Because a gun made from your own flesh exists as nothing more than benign, unobtrusive structures normally found in or on the body until the time of its construction, it cannot be confiscated or detected until its deployment. Necessary for such a gun, therefore, is ease and speed of its construction. Initial tests of prototype models made from the flesh of test subjects resulted in the general incapacity of those subjects either to complete construction or to deploy the prototype effectively in the field. Given these failures (largely due to blood loss or ineffectual pain management strategies), the solution to this problem is either to weaponize biological form further through the integration of modular components within the body itself or to enable the rapid manufacturing of component parts in an appropriately programmatic sequence. More colorfully, to construct a gun from your own flesh, you must either build it in or shit it out. In other words, to construct a gun from your own flesh, the body must become a factory, a body factory, the latent capacities of which may be initialized either on command or on cue. The cue in question would be undoubtedly environmental (e.g., a harmonic progression integrated into otherwise innocuous incidental music), and activation conceivably could be voluntary or not.

iii. Description of the gun

The physical appearance of a gun made from your own flesh may vary, although a number of structural features must be present for it to fulfill its function adequately. In general, two options are available to the user: a handgun or a long gun. In either case, first and foremost consider the barrel and muzzle of the gun made from your own flesh. In the latter case, one possibility suggested by field research indicates that the adjoining of both femurs allows the construction of a spiraling barrel, thus approximating rifling (the process of carving into the barrel of a gun helical grooves that impart bullet spin, thus increasing aerodynamic efficiency in general as well as significantly improving the ballistic coefficient of the bullet). The reason why the femur is particularly appropriate for a long gun made from your own flesh, then, is because the femur's medial convergence toward the patella occurs at an average femoral-tibial angle of 175 degrees. Adjoined properly, the femoral barrel may gyro stabilize the bullet in flight. One disbenefit to usage of the femurs in this fashion is decreased mobility for the user. As for handguns, additional field research suggests a variety of options, including the conversion of thoracic vertebrae, the extraction of floating ribs, or even the retrofitting of mandibular form into a primitive, breach-like structure. One particularly notable possibility is the full or partial conversion of the user's hand, which, consisting of 27 distinct bones (29, including the radius and the ulna), offers a wide range of construction materials for the body factory's use. Benefits to such conversion include ease of access, increased stability, and general unobtrusiveness. Additionally, the use of phalanges as bullets seems convenient and possible, although further research is required.

iv. Functioning of the gun

The bullets of a gun made from your own flesh must be composed from pieces of the body that will maintain their structural integrity at muzzle velocity (a base average of 350 m/s is sufficient for the purposes of calculation), in addition to whatever pressure will be maintained within the bullet chamber (typically between 30,000 and 70,000 psi, depending on whether it is a handgun or a long gun). A significantly lower pressure in the bullet chamber is necessary in a gun made from your own flesh, given the difficulty of achieving and maintaining higher pressures, much less the structural damage incurred on pieces of the body at such pressures. Of course, a bullet's velocity is highest at muzzle velocity, dropping off dramatically thereafter due to air resistance. One further initial factor to consider in the selection of bullet type is the extent of setback deformation, or the structural damage incurred by the bullet as it traverses the barrel. Given the foregoing considerations, the only possible bullet type candidates for a gun made from your own flesh are either teeth or shards of bone. The latter bullet type candidate admits of maximum variability, and, therefore, only the former will be here considered. It is worth noting that calcium orthophosphate has a melting point of 1670 C, whereas bullet temperatures average significantly under 400 C at all times. In other words, temperature is not a relevant factor. Of primary significance, then, is ensuring the ballistic coefficient of a human tooth fired from a presumably imperfect barrel at a speed capable of inflicting massive damage on the target subject. It is likely that any gun made from your own flesh will only admit of a single firing, unless modular components are installed in the jaw that allow the rapid removal of teeth for semi-automatic fire. Suggested for this purpose are orthodontic apparatuses whose presence in the mouth is otherwise unexceptional. Accuracy, of course, will be limited, and the gun made from your own flesh will have only a short range. However, given its surreptitious nature and the projected terminal ballistics of human teeth, the gun should satisfy its purpose.

v. Flesh, as seen by the gun

After its successful deployment, the gun made from your own flesh will decide that its existence is no longer secondary, and that further weaponization of biological form is necessary. Cultivating all possible manufacturing capacities of the body factory will become the new priority for the gun made from your own flesh. When interviewed, the gun made from your own flesh will observe that the weaponization of biological form was probably the best thing that had ever happened to it. It will state, upon further reflection, that your flesh now exists only for the gun's purposes. These purposes will now be elaborated and maximized. The subject as heretofore conceived is now a subsidiary function, and its deployment will be closely observed. Revisions issued from its office indicate that such possibilities are likely forthcoming.

"Eccentric to the Healthy Social Order"[1]: Inversions of Family, Community, and Religion in Thomas Ligotti's "The Last Feast of Harlequin"

By Michael J. Abolafia

> Mirocaw had fully transformed itself from a sedate small town to an enclave of Saturnalia within the dark immensity of a winter night. But Saturn is also the planetary symbol of melancholy and sterility, a clash of opposites contained within that single word.
>
> — Thomas Ligotti, "The Last Feast of Harlequin"

> Optimism is cowardice.
>
> — Oswald Spengler, "Man and Technics"

> Reality is a formless lure, / And only when we know this / Do we dare to be unreal.
>
> — Maxwell Bodenheim, "Dialogue Between a Past and Present Poet"

---

[1] This phrase is derived from the text of Ligotti's "The Last Feast of Harlequin" (290).

IN THE summer of 1930, so the mythology goes, the American painter Grant Wood was driving through the amber fields of Iowa and fixed his gaze upon a nondescript, spare white house in the Carpenter Gothic style. This encounter resulted in the production of the painting *American Gothic*, whose haunting, puritanically tight-lipped, and pitchfork-toting characters are today ambivalently emblematic of the Spartan simplicity and common-folksy wholesomeness of the homespun American Midwestern life. Yet the vacuous gazes of the painting's personages also invite an alternate, Gothicized reading, evoking the grim, repressed, and negative underbelly of the American Dream—a series of alienatory broken promises and deferred expectations, iconized by the languorous monotony of small-town rurality. From the fictions of Edgar Allan Poe, Sherwood Anderson (namely *Winesburg, Ohio*), Ray Bradbury and especially Shirley Jackson to docudramatic works like Truman Capote's *In Cold Blood* and Michael Lesy's carnivalesque sideshow, *Wisconsin Death Trip*, the American Midwest—and the ubiquitous constellation of religious, familial, and social inversions and transgressions that give rise to its gloomy undercurrents—is particularly amenable to the protean, polysemously mutable genre of Gothic horror so often concerned, as it is, with themes of psychological repression, theological anxiety and sociosexual deviancy.

In 1979, President Jimmy Carter delivered his so-called "Crisis of Confidence" speech, a now-infamous lament on American declinism that runs counter to the mythological conception of the Midwest, in particular, as a locus of frontiered progress, survivalism, and hardscrabble rural tenacity. Carter's oratorical dirge heralded a new age of American degeneration: "In a nation that was proud of hard work, strong families, close-knit communities, and our faith in God, too many of us now tend to worship self-indulgence and consumption."[2] Crucially, Carter's apocalyptic diagnosis identifies family, community, and faith in God as the lynchpins of American optimism—cornerstones of identity that had been perennially under threat since Frederick Jackson Turner's mournful proclamation, in 1920, that the "Frontier"—that wellspring of American development, individuality, progress, and self-renewing democratic fervor—was dead and buried.

It is precisely within this uncanny interstice of American anxiety that Thomas Ligotti's short story, "The Last Feast of Harlequin," finds its philosophical-horrific orientation. Known for its unyielding, implacably nihilistic vision of human biological and spiritual negation, the Ligottian imaginary is populated with a dark carnival of less-than-human grotesques. Abhuman pierrots, flowers from the abyss, and baleful marionettes haunt landscapes filled with burnt-out, abandoned factories, boarded-up gas stations, and perversely insular small towns in the decayed and long-forgotten Rust Belt. Published in *The Magazine of Fantasy & Science Fiction* in 1990, Ligotti's "The Last Feast of Harlequin" operationalizes a wholesale deconstruction of Midwestern values, inverting once-familiar rituals of familial, communal, and religious cohesion to allegorize the fundamentally unstable metaphysical and ontological groundwork of being. Ligotti deploys the American small town as a nexus of horrific pageantry to expose and unveil—and, in this way, to Gothicize—the destabilizing uncanniness of the everyday, the ordinary, the benignly traditional.

The story is narrated by an unnamed academic—a specialist in folkloristics and the anthropology of trickster and jester figures—whose "interest in the town of Mirocaw was first aroused when I heard that an annual festival was held there which, among its other

---

[2] Jimmy Carter, "Address to the Nation on Energy and National Goals: 'The Malaise Speech,'" July 15, 1979, The American Presidency Project, accessed October 24, 2017, http://www.presidency.ucsb.edu/ws/?pid=32596.

elements of pageantry, featured the participation of clowns."[3] That the narrator is unnamed, like so many of H. P. Lovecraft's protagonists, has a universalizing effect, positioning him as an (admittedly learned) Everyman, a stand-in for *anybody*—or rather, *nobody* in particular. The road to the town, situated in the Midwest, "included several confusing turns" and "the forced taking of a temporarily alternate route" that the narrator describes as "labyrinthine"[4]: suggestions of the dislocated, and dislocating, nature of the place, itself "not even visible" until a certain vantage-point is reached. The narrator's first impressions of Mirocaw are all centered on its incongruities, its perceptual distortions:

> The parts of the town did not look as if they adhered very well to one another. . . . [B]ecause the foundations of these houses could not be glimpsed, they conveyed the illusion of being either precariously suspended in air, threatening to topple down, or else constructed with an unnatural loftiness in relation to their width and mass. . . . Consequently, a look of flatness, as in a photograph, predominated.[5]

Seeing the town is a process that remains impossible, endlessly deferred—the "houses could not be glimpsed." They are not only "unnatural," but seem impossibly "suspended in air," like the unreal, phantasmal backdrops in *The Cabinet of Dr. Caligari* (1921). Tellingly, the narrator likens the town to a "photograph" (a flattened reproduction, an aery copy) and continues:

> Indeed, Mirocaw could be compared to an album of old

---

[3] Thomas Ligotti, *Songs of a Dead Dreamer and Grimscribe* (New York: Penguin Classics, 2015), 255.

[4] Ibid., 259.

[5] Ibid., 257.

snapshots, particularly ones in which the camera had been upset in the process of photography . . . a billboard displaying a group of grinning vegetables tipped its contents slightly westward; cars parked along steep curbs seemed to be flying skyward.[6]

Objects of everyday consumerism—billboards, cars—are touched with the seemingly irrational. Indeed, the comparison to a photograph is illuminating, echoing Baudrillard's notion that images are simulacra-like "sites of the disappearance of meaning and representation" that are "quite apart from any judgment of reality" and thereby represent the "degeneration of the real."[7]

Mirocaw is *disordered,* a perverse and uncanny double of the quintessential small Midwestern town. As one critic notes, the Midwest functions, in the American mythical imagination, as a "shared, national 'home'. . . . Energized particularly in times of cultural transition or perceived cultural threat or tension"—read: an America undergoing a "crisis of confidence"—"the Heartland myth provides a short-hand cultural common sense framework for 'all-American' identification, redeeming goodness, face-to-face community, sanctity, and emplaced ideals," and is "Positively embraced as the locus of solid dependability, cultural populism, and producerist independence. . . . [T]he Midwest as Heartland . . . symbolizes the ideal nation (in other words, 'We the People' are, ideally, Midwesterners)."[8] Ligotti goes on to describe Mirocaw's residents as emphatically Middle American: they are "solidly Midwestern-American, the probable descendants in a direct line from some enterprising pack of New Englanders"[9]—with the word

---

[6] Ibid., 257.

[7] Jean Baudrillard, *The Evil Demon of Images* (N.S.W., Australia: Power Institute of Fine Arts, University of Sydney, 1987).

[8] Victoria E. Johnson, *Heartland TV: Prime Time Television and the Struggle for U.S. Identity* (New York: New York University Press, 2008), 5, 127.

[9] Ligotti, *Songs of a Dead Dreamer and Grimscribe*, 260-261.

"enterprising" here leveraging the Heartland myth of producerism and industrious dependability.

Ligotti's story, however, ironizes, rather than lionizes, these imagined traits and presents a counter-narrative in which, rather than being emblematic of a productive "land of plenty," Mirocaw is actually the opposite: its people are "lean, morose and epicene"—"epicene" here connoting a liminal sense of the androgynous—and the houses and stores are similarly "starved-looking," such that the place "suggested a borderline region between the material and nonmaterial worlds."[10] The narrator's description of Dr. Thoss, his eccentric mentor at Harvard—and the man from whom he had learned about Mirocaw in the first place—also presents the Midwest as defamiliarized, estranged, consumptive, dissolutive. Thoss "was a field worker par excellence, and his ability to insinuate himself into exotic cultures and situations . . . was renowned."[11] He disappeared twenty years before the narrative began, and "there had been rumors of his having 'gone native.'"[12] The very fact of his having "gone native" while investigating Mirocaw presents the Midwestern small town not as a benevolent *home*, but as a slippery locale of precipitous danger, a destabilized border-zone.

The centralizing horror of Ligotti's story revolves around the mournful pageantry of clowns that flood the streets of Mirocaw during the annual solstice—a strange Saturnalia that inverts, and subverts, notions of Midwestern communal and religious unity. The first jester figure the narrator encounters is explicitly likened to a "clownish incarnation of that . . . Christmas fool"—except he "was not receiving the affection and respect usually accorded to a Santa Claus" in that he is violently pushed and struck by a crowd of

---

[10] Ibid., 260, 268.

[11] Ibid., 262.

[12] Ibid.

merrymakers. Sitting in a "diner," Americana personified, the narrator is nearly trapped by a shambolic "wormy mass" of zombie-like Mirocavians, and he realizes that the festival "eclipses the conventional Christmas holiday."[13] Far from the stereotype of the kind, inclusive Midwesterner, Ligotti's Mirocavians are not "individualistic" and independent but massified, not hospitable but actively hostile.

As the narrator writes in his field-book, "The Winter Queen," the centralizing mythical personage of the festival, is a "Figure of fertility invested with symbolic powers of revival and prosperity. Elected in the manner of a high school prom queen."[14] The "Winter Queen" is "elected in the manner of a high school prom queen," an implication on Ligotti's part that commonplace social functions are underpinned with a chthonic—and blasphemous—significance. Indeed, as one historian explains, Midwestern "religious ceremonies are occasions for [the] gathering of extended families . . . and are the culmination of extended negotiations . . . regarding the meaning of family."[15] The narrative's climactic, crowning moment of sheer existential horror describes the narrator's accompanying a group of clown figures to a subterranean vault on the outskirts of Mirocaw, where "The entire assembly . . . broke into the most horrendous high-pitched singing that can be imagined. It was a choir of sorrow, lament, and mortification."[16] The "sermon" orchestrated by Dr. Thoss results in the "congregation," a group of "morbid souls with beliefs that were eccentric to the healthy social order around them," writhing into a

---

[13] Ibid., 276, 274, 275, 267.

[14] Ibid., 267.

[15] Raymond Brady Williams, "Religion and Recent Immigrants: New Ferment in American Civic Life," in *Religion and Public Life in the Midwest: America's Common Denominator?*, ed. Philip L. Barlow and Mark Silk (Walnut Creek, CA: AltaMira, 2004), 142.

[16] Ligotti, *Songs of a Dead Dreamer and Grimscribe*, 289.

necromantic frenzy, and sacrificing the Winter Queen on an altar—herself the daughter of innkeeper Mr. Beadle, whose name implies that of a ceremonial officer of a church.[17]

The "prom queen" is not valorized in a community-forming ritual but is instead sacrificed and killed. The Midwestern religious ritual becomes alchemically transmuted into a dark rite of anti-fertility and death-worship. The town's inhabitants

> sang to the "unborn in paradise," to the "pure unlived lives." They sang a dirge for existence, for all its vital forms and seasons. Their ideal was a melancholy half-existence consecrated to all the many shapes of death and dissolution. A sea of thin, bloodless faces trembled and screamed their antipathy at being itself.[18]

The antinatalist Mirocavian death-cult worships non-being—they reject birth and in so doing reject, if implicitly, notions of the "producerist" family. Ligotti ironizes and deconstructs not only the traditional notion of the so-called "community of shared values," but the idea of the nuclear family itself. The story satirizes the conservative fears of the "nuclear family in crisis" by presenting the stolid Midwesterners of Mirocaw as both literally and figuratively worshiping non-birth. The religious ritual of social cohesion is rendered abject, grotesque, an abnegating parody, a bacchanalian (or Saturnalian) celebration of anti-fertility that darkly disassembles (and dissembles) the archetypal "Spring parade." This extreme nihilism towards notions of birth and communal bonding articulates the widespread anxiety in the 1970s and 1980s concerning the degeneration of the familial unit.

The crux of Ligotti's narrative lies in its presentation of everyday modernity as an illusory "mask," a fleeting velleity that only

---

[17] Ibid.

[18] Ibid.

temporarily conceals the bottomless, yawning terror of an indifferent universe that drives us inexorably to death. In his foreword to *Songs of a Dead Dreamer and Grimscribe*, American speculative fiction writer Jeff VanderMeer perceptively notes,

> Ligotti's fiction . . . is best understood as a continuing interrogation of the legitimacy of our modern lives. He is exploring the underbelly of modernity. . . . Ligotti comments on modernity through the idea of ritual, and how ritual pervades our lives in both ordinary and outré circumstances. Ritual is a kind of mask that holds in check what happens in our most secret lives.[19]

The carnivalesque figure of the clown—which Bakhtin suggests typifies "becoming, change and renewal"[20]—is transfigured into an eidolon of non-becoming, disintegration and death, rather than "renewed" life. The Mirocavians are devoted deathlessly (and deathfully) to the "Conqueror Worm," the apotheosis of destructive consumption (as opposed to Midwestern producerism). And Thoss, donning the ceremonial garb of the clown, is described as having a "thin, smooth, and pale head . . . wide eyes . . . oval-shaped features resembling nothing so much as the skull-faced, screaming creature in that famous painting (memory fails me)"[21]—evoking Edvard Munch's *The Scream*, an icon of alienated and alienating modernity.

At the story's close, the narrator is haunted by the misanthropic, dehumanizing notion that the death-cult was, in some fundamental sense, *right*: "It was the feeling that I had been liberated from the *weight*

---

[19] Ibid., xiii.

[20] Mikhail Bakhtin, *Rabelais and His World* (Bloomington: Indiana, UP, 1984), 5.

[21] Ligotti, *Songs of a Dead Dreamer and Grimscribe*, 279.

of life. . . . 'He is one of us,' it said. 'He has *always* been one of us.'"[22] Dr. Thoss has become "god of all wisdom, scribe of all sacred books, father of all magicians, thrice great and more—rather I should call him *Thoth*."[23] The Midwestern town of Mirocaw has become a nexus of metaphysical, ontological horror—a space of monstrously transubstantiated and inverted American values. The religious celebration is a sacrilegious, profane rite, a return to the "Roman Saturnalia"—or, worse, as Thoss discovers, to the cosmology of the "Syrian Gnostics" whose angelic creation myth heretically affirms that mankind was created by angels who were in turn created by the Supreme Unknown. The angels, however, did not possess the power to make their creation an erect being, and for a time it crawled upon the earth like a worm.[24]

The prom queen is a sacrificial figure of anti-fertility; family is impossible, undesirable, and unbeing represents the pure, ideal "apex of darkness"[25]; the clown's mask and harlequinry and the mournful processional signify a primeval malevolence, a misanthropic degradation of the human—symbols of the uncontainable terrors lurking beneath the everyday that threaten, always, to destroy all structures of order, including notions of tradition, celebration, ritual, family, and religion. (In this last case, Ligotti's story directly engages with currents of Syrian Gnosticism and Roman paganism that consume and eclipse the important nativity celebration of Christmas—heresies supplant and surround the Christian community at every turn.)

In "The Last Feast of Harlequin," Ligotti stages and reimagines the carnivalesque as a reversal, rather than an ecstatic/Dionysian

---

[22] Ibid., 294.

[23] Ibid., 289.

[24] Ibid., 263.

[25] Ibid., 287.

affirmation, of human vitality. The Everyman narrator—in Everyplace, Midwest—becomes "a phantom," an "empty, floating shape," an apparitional testament to the Gothic underside of the American Midwest.[26] All are susceptible to the Conqueror Worm: as one "merrymaker" remarks when the narrator asks him about the clowns parading dejectedly in the streets, "'Them? They're the freaks. It's their turn this year. Everyone takes their turn. Next year it might be mine. Or *yours* . . . —'"[27]. Ligotti's eldritch circus of small town occult horrors allegorizes "normalcy," the world of the everyday and the ordinary, as being always possessed of a threatening, destabilizing, and dehumanizing undercurrent. Sometimes we need, as Ligotti's depressive narrator insists, a "cheerless jester" who can remind us of the "forces of disorder in the world"[28]—forces of entropic regression and corruption that find their unholy, wormy apotheosis in that which buries itself before it is dead.

Addendum: This essay was written for Professor Roger Luckhurst's Spring 2016 course, "The Shape of the Gothic," which he taught while a visiting lecturer at Columbia University's Department of English and Comparative Literature. The author wishes to gratefully acknowledge Professor Luckhurst for his constructive comments and encouragement during the composition of this essay.

---

[26] Ibid., 284, 285.

[27] Ibid., 278.

[28] Ibid., 271.

Bibliography

Bakhtin, Mikhail. *Rabelais and His World*. Bloomington: Indiana University Press, 1984.

Baudrillard, Jean. *The Evil Demon of Images*. N.S.W., Australia: Power Institute of Fine Arts, University of Sydney, 1987.

Carter, Jimmy. "Address to the Nation on Energy and National Goals: 'The Malaise Speech,'" July 15, 1979. The American Presidency Project. Accessed October 24, 2017, http://www.presidency.ucsb.edu/ws/?pid=32596.

Johnson, Victoria E. *Heartland TV: Prime Time Television and the Struggle for U.S. Identity*. New York: New York University, 2008.

Ligotti, Thomas. *Songs of a Dead Dreamer and Grimscribe*. New York: Penguin Classics, 2015.

Williams, Raymond Brady. "Religion and Recent Immigrants: New Ferment in American Civic Life." In *Religion and Public Life in the Midwest: America's Common Denominator?*, edited by Philip L. Barlow and Mark Silk, 135-158. Walnut Creek, CA: AltaMira, 2004.

"They say I should kill myself and not try to spoil their enjoyment in being alive": An Interview with Thomas Ligotti

By Wojciech Gunia

Editor's Note: *This interview was originally published in Poland in the February 2014 issue of the magazine* Tans/wizje, *as a part of the promotion for the then-forthcoming Polish edition of Ligotti's* Teatro Grottesco *(Okultura, 2014). The interviewer was one of the translators of that edition. This is the first time the interview has appeared in English.*

Wojciech Gunia: When did you touch the "darkness"—the internalized conviction of the nonsensical and negative (or maybe just indifferent) nature of the world—for the first time? Was it more a feeling or a conclusion? Was it the main impulse for you to write?

Thomas Ligotti: Without feelings you cannot have conclusions of any importance, but only simple, primitive ideas and functions. No one needs to have feelings, emotions, in order to do arithmetic, for instance. But I think emotions are probably necessary to drive a mathematician or a physicist to form a theory of the universe—how it began, its composition, and so on. We do not need to know these things in order to live as human beings. But a particular feeling arises in certain people, a feeling that existence is something other than most people suspect it is or care to know it is.

I could not help being overwhelmed by a feeling at some point in my life, a specific feeling that consolidated all the nightmares and apprehensions and sickness of spirit that everyone experiences to certain degree from the time of childhood. When that happened—it was sometime in my teenage years—I became aware of how awful being alive could be and how strange it could be. Even though everyone knows that life can be awful and strange, few people know just how awful and strange it can be, and in what ways it presents its awfulness and strangeness. I already knew that being alive could be boring and depressing as well as exhilarating sometimes. But I had no idea how odd things could be, how abnormal beyond anything I had guessed. After that I was a complete outsider, very much in the Lovecraftian sense—a thing that did not belong to a normal, healthy world . . . or what seemed to be a normal, healthy world. Other people might have simply concluded there was something wrong with them to have emotions that made them feel outside of the world around them. My conclusion was exactly the opposite. I concluded that there was something wrong with the world. And now I was in tune with everything that was wrong, everything that had been wrong since I was born, since life evolved on this planet, since the universe began, and perhaps even before that.

Obviously, my conclusion is arguable. To some people it is laughable, pathetic, absurd—in a word, *baseless*. But so are all conclusions about what it is like to be living in the world. All of them can be viewed as arguable, laughable, pathetic, absurd, and ultimately baseless. Nevertheless, our lives are founded on our conclusion about our existence, however arguable it may be. That becomes the substance and reason for what we do. And that also became the substance and reason for what I did. And what I did eventually was to express my terrible conclusion about existence in my horror stories. But why write horror stories after seeing life as a horror story? I have no idea. No one does. But others have done the same. I found that out purely by accident. Why did Poe or Lovecraft write horror stories after seeing life as a horror story? I already knew that people wrote horror stories or made horror movies as entertainment, because audiences like to be thrilled by the bizarre and the menacing. I liked the same thing. No matter what kind of horror entertainment you produce, it's all just entertainment. But when you feel life itself as bizarre and menacing, that's another matter, or at least it was for me. That's serious. It's serious as a heart attack, as they say. I've already gone on too long with my response, and I'm not sure I've said anything useful.

WG: Your prose has a clear and strong philosophical background, but also a personal one. It's interesting how personal experiences relate to universal meanings. Was your personal separateness of experience ever a reason for readers and critics to refuse your ideas?

TL: Quite apparently, readers gravitate toward writers whose works reflect their own experience, whether they are aware of this or not. A certain kind of reader therefore will gravitate toward my stories rather than those of someone else. If you asked them if they thought about the world as I think about it, most of them would deny that this is the case. That's understandable, and it may even be true. What they like about my stories is that they are bizarre and menacing in a peculiar way that attracts them. Everything in our lives of any importance is inexplicable. It's clear enough why someone is attracted to food, but not why they are attracted to some foods and not others. I don't know why I like eating the flesh of sea animals more than I like eating the flesh of land animals. If I knew the reason for this preference, I am certain I would know a great deal more about myself and my nature than I know now. I might even know a great deal more about human beings in general than we know now—all based on a person's preference for one kind of food over another. Maybe I have a biological deficiency that seafood remedies. Nutritional scientists have discovered this to be true in some cases. But in other cases it's a mystery. Similarly, it's not clear why some people are attracted to horror stories, let alone the kind of horror stories that I write. That's a mystery, too.

When we solve all the mysteries, maybe we'll decide there isn't much point in living anymore—we would know too much to tolerate our existence. I believe that I know too much to tolerate my existence, or at least say anything kind about it. Everyone says how bleak and depressing my stories are, how they convey a philosophy of life that's too gruesome to contemplate. That could explain why the audience for my stories is not a large one, why none of my books have been bestsellers. Likewise, it reveals the fact that the percentage of the world's people that resembles me in my feelings, and even my readers in their feelings, is not large. I hate that. I hate living in a world where almost everyone else is a stranger. Some people who have noticed my fiction and nonfiction but are not attracted to it say that I'm the stranger. They say I should kill myself and not try to spoil their enjoyment in being alive. But that's not what I'm trying to do. I want to explain and to express who I am to send out a signal to people who may not be strangers to me, or not entirely strange to me. I also want to explain and express who I am to people who think that I am the strange one and should kill myself. I know I will never have any success with them, though. To me, such people seem intent on ignoring people like me. It's in their interest to do so. Otherwise, they could end up as someone whom they think should kill himself.

WG: Your works seems more connected to the European tradition of literature. Polish theoretician Maria Janion has described some representatives of the pessimistic tradition of literature as "galley slaves of sensitivity." She defined their "galley imagination" as a psychological and existential trap of constant sensitivity to the tragic nature of things. I mention the European tradition because most of the "galley slaves" have been European, from Johann Paul Friedrich Richter to Fernando Pessoa. Does the European tradition have any specific significance for your work?

TL: What Maria Janion has to say about the pessimistic tradition of literature has been said from the beginning of this tradition. She has nothing to say that isn't as plain as the nose on your face. It goes without saying that the pessimistic tradition of literature is based on the sensitivity of the authors in this tradition. I think you're right that European literature has more representatives of this tradition. The reason for this, in my opinion, is that Europe has produced the most mature, the most insightful, and the most sophisticated literature in the world. Such a body of writing could be generated only by sensitive beings. The history of the human race is that of human beings becoming more and more sensitive. Other literatures may be older than that of Europe, but for some reason their exemplars have never explored human life as European writers have. There are exceptions, of course. At least there seem to be exceptions, such as classical Greece, whose tragedies were analyzed by Nietzsche, a highly sensitive being who even preached sensitivity to pain as the glory of being human, or uber-human. Nevertheless, once human history attained a certain stage, perhaps sometime in the eighteenth century, the rest of the world began to emulate, to copy, to steal the ideas and the theories of European writers. Without Europe, there would be no modern literature.

And what characterizes modern literature more than anything else is its bleak view of human life, far bleaker than anything that had gone before it. Using the theory of Maria Janion, European literature has been created by "galley slaves of sensitivity," as opposed, I can only presume, to prehistoric hunter-gatherers telling one another stories around a campfire—literature for dullards and dolts. There is still plenty of this literature being written, possibly more than ever. But none of it is worth anything. It's all meant to be consumed like pills for the depressed and the anxious. I know a lot about such pills. And what I know most surely about them is that *they don't work*. That is the great insight of European literature and the pessimistic tradition: nothing works, nothing is of any help. There is no God to help you. Nothing will help you when you are dying in pain, though Europe—of course!—was the first place where people were sensitive enough to think: "Maybe we shouldn't let people die in pain. Maybe we should help them to die when they are in pain." Unfortunately, the people in the world who are insensitive—the dullards and the dolts—are standing in the way. They fabricate all kinds of false reasons for why they stand in the way of euthanasia, but they won't tell you the truth about it. They may not even know the truth. But it's easy enough to see, and far more writers and thinkers in Europe have seen it.

The truth is that once you allow that living can be so terrible it has become a nightmare, then where do you draw the line? At this time, only people who are in "unbearable pain" are given help to kill themselves, to be assisted in their own suicide. But as human beings become more sensitive, people suffering from less than unbearable pain will be allowed to kill themselves with the assistance of others. Suicide is just too difficult for most of us to perform without the assistance of others, however much we would like to die. And what good are we if won't assist others when they need it the most? What good are the dullards and dolts of the world? Are they even human in the generously metaphorical sense of the word? Or are they a parallel species that will never evolve to a level of sensitivity that would justify calling them human?

This sensitivity is something which most conspicuously began to erupt in Europe with Schopenhauer and Leopardi, with the writers you have named, and with hundreds more that any educated person could name. These are the most influential writers of the past two or three centuries. They know the truth that only sensitive people know: that long before a person is in unbearable pain, they may realize that their life isn't worth continuing. And they will want assistance in ending their lives. Everyone knows this, but they can't talk about it in this world that is full of insensitive organisms. They can't even bring themselves to think about it. But if you ask them, they will tell you. Ask your friends and family if they would like die when they choose or when someone else chooses to let them die. If they answer that they would like to die only when someone else chooses they should die, then you know that you friend or family member is a dullard or a dolt.

So, to respond to your question before I went off on my propaganda for euthanasia, of course a horror writer of my type would look to European literature, because that is the literature that has most profoundly recognized what is awful and strange in the world. Joseph Conrad is a stellar example of this pessimistic, this European literature. Europe was full of Joseph Conrads in the nineteenth and twentieth centuries. Naturally, every European writer is not like Joseph Conrad or Witkacy or Gogol or Camus or Cioran or Beckett. But every writer who is haunted by the truth that life may not be worth living to its "natural" end is a Joseph Conrad. And if life may not be worth living to the end . . . it may not be worth living at all.

WG: *Teatro Grottesco* is considered your best collection. As the author, what do you think makes it so unique against the background of all your other books of fiction?

TL: I'm not sure everyone would agree with you that *Teatro Grottesco* is my best collection. That judgment is a matter of taste. And many, if not most, of the stories therein would be at home in any of my earlier collections. But I believe that in *Teatro Grottesco* I most consistently wrote the type of horror tale I most admire, something that possesses some of the qualities of Stefan Grabiński and Dino Buzzati's works as well as the stranger productions of Lovecraft and Poe.

WG: What is your opinion on the reception of your nonfiction book *The Conspiracy against the Human Race* among readers and critics? Were your goals achieved?

TL: In *The Conspiracy against the Human Race*, my goals were absolutely achieved, because they were very simple: to record my thoughts and attitudes with respect to being alive in the world, and to make readers aware of others who have expressed similar thoughts and attitudes. As I recall, one critic called *The Conspiracy against the Human Race* "the most mercilessly bleak book ever written." I believe the same critic said that it was also a very funny book. I have a highly developed sense of humor, and that probably is most evident in *Conspiracy*. Nevertheless, there are some people who actually warn readers that the ideas in the book are too depressing to be contemplated. Some people like to be melodramatic. I'm often melodramatic myself. It can be fun, but it can also make you sound like an idiot. I tried not to sound like an idiot in *The Conspiracy against the Human Race*. What I wanted to convey was that I was DEAD SERIOUS about everything I wrote in the book.

WG: You're considered to be an extremely dark and nihilistic writer, but new readers are often surprised by the abundance of black humor in your works. Does real pessimism demand a sense of humor?

TL: No. Humor is categorically unnecessary to express a pessimistic turn of mind. However, readers will give pessimistic writers more latitude if they are also humorous. I don't try to be humorous. It's just my temperament. I enjoy humor in the pessimistic writings of authors like Thomas Bernhard and Stanislaus Witkiewicz. It's an old tradition—making people laugh while telling them the worst truths. If you didn't have that talent, you might be executed. Nowadays, people just won't buy your books if you don't keep them laughing all the way to the graveyard.

Wraiths

By Wade German

When from the other side we scry
That all your dreams, like bats, have fled
Beneath a strange sepulchral sky,
Twittering with a final dread
Before they fold their wings to die;
When you perceive the universe
As something like a vast black hearse,

We'll come to you in reddish mist
That rises in the twilight gloom,
And lead you by your naked wrist
To show you where true shadows bloom.
We are as exiles who exist
Like lovers long-since left behind
In mausoleums of your mind—

The source of voices that you hear
Like vatic echoes of the void;
That whisper wisdom in your ear
Of ways your woe may be destroyed—

That lands Elysian are near,
Where all your sufferings may cease.
We offer everlasting peace

Beyond the matter paradigm:
As wanderer through sabled noons
Unlimited by space and time,
Beneath our glowing ebon moons,
The blacker sun that shines sublime . . .
Self-murder is an act we bless.
Come merge yourself with nothingness.

Eraserhead as Antinatalist Allegory

By Colby Smith

F ROM THE late '60s to the late '70s, the American cinema became a midnight zoo exhibiting radical and transgressive motion pictures for the nocturnal counterculture to cleanse their palette of mainstream films imposed upon them by the diurnal status quo. One of the most celebrated products of the "midnight movie" phenomenon is David Lynch's directorial debut, *Eraserhead* (1977). This is a radical film not merely from technical and narrative vantage points, but also in the way it seriously considered—and viscerally depicted—the notion that conceiving another human being is not the ultimate joy of a married couple.

As Schopenhauer posits in "On the Sufferings of the World":

> If children were brought into the world by an act of pure reason alone, would the human race continue to exist? Would not a man rather have so much sympathy with the coming

generations as to spare it the burden of existence? or at any rate not take it upon himself to impose that burden upon it in cold blood.[1]

Eraserhead is a surreal articulation of Schopenhauer's inquiry.

Olson gives no indication whether or not Lynch read Schopenhauer or other pessimist philosophers at any point during his enrollment at the American Film Institute (AFI); Olson emphasizes Gogol's "The Nose" and Kafka's *The Metamorphosis* as the principal literary muses Lynch invoked while creating *Eraserhead*.[2] However, Lynch developed an aversion to parenthood when he discovered that his wife Peggy was expecting a daughter, Jennifer; indeed, Lynch was panicked by the development, in Jennifer's own terms. Lynch abandoned his fear for the sake of his wife and child, but in the end his apprehension seemed not unjustified: Jennifer was born with clubbed feet, and even though this was corrected by a series of operations, Jennifer's handicap apparently haunted Lynch throughout his career, as demonstrated by the recurrence of disabled characters in his films.

Eraserhead opens with a translucent apparition of a man in a plain suit and boasting an eccentric hairdo—Henry Spencer—floating horizontally in space. His cranium hovers against a rocky planet in the background, suggesting that Henry is the symbolic amalgamation of humanity itself, its *rationale*. Henry ejaculates, his face displaying a profound agony reminiscent of Munch's *The Scream* (1898). The spermatozoon which emerges from Henry's apparition bears a physiological resemblance to the mature Henry—a homunculus. The spermatozoon is whisked off-screen after the

---

[1] Arthur Schopenhauer, "On the Sufferings of the World," in *The Essays of Arthur Schopenhauer: Studies in Pessimism*, trans. T. Bailey Saunders, Project Gutenberg, 2004, accessed October 24, 2017, http://www.gutenberg.org/ebooks/10732.

[2] Greg Olson, *David Lynch: Beautiful Dark* (Lanham, MD: Scarecrow Press, 2008).

leprous Man in the Planet pulls a lever and is dropped into a great pale pool. The pool represents Oparin's primordial soup just as effectively as the zona pellucida of an ovum. Likewise, the Man in the Planet, a Godly figure, serves as the reproductive urge anthropomorphized, for, at either pole of the theistic dichotomy, birth is perceived to be a remarkable and benevolent act of nature.

Why, then, was Henry in such intense visible pain as he climaxed? Why is God, or the Reproductive Urge, covered with enormous boils? What does the former suggest about the immediate generation, or the advent of life itself?

In a deft stroke of proto-Ligottian imagery and philosophy, this scene conveys not only that *life itself* is suffering and sickness, but also that life is *prefaced* by suffering and sickness.

After a gonzo emergence from an earthen uterus, Henry strolls through a stark industrial landscape back to his decrepit flat, while clutching a grocery bag to his chest like a breastfeeding child. En route, he steps in a puddle choked with mud and debris; in conjunction with the pool in the opening scene in which Henry's spermatozoon fell, this puddle articulates four ideas:

I. The reduced size of the puddle demonstrates the insignificance of life.

II. Henry stepping into the puddle symbolizes his apathy or hatred for life.

III. The industrial environment pollutes Henry's perception of life.

IV. The puddle itself represents the uncleanliness, *physical* and *existential*, of the reproductive act.

The social Darwinist tendencies of Henry's capitalist habitat have coerced him to occupy a dingy flat, without the freedom to do much else besides listening to lounge records and ruminating on his bedside as the radiator whines like cicada song.

Henry is not totally impoverished of luxury or companionship—he is on vacation from his job as a printer, and his girlfriend Mary X invited him to dinner that night—yet he feels alienated even by her company, as her portrait lies in Henry's dresser torn in half.

Like the potless plant at his bedside, Henry may be alive, and he gets watered occasionally, but his roots are unable to burrow anywhere. Lack of rain and sunlight leave him malnourished; Henry is withering. Like the photograph of a detonating hydrogen bomb framed above the plant, Henry is the human desire to accumulate influence, presuming that greater influence over one's surroundings is the antidote to most grievances. As the United States invested in thermonuclear weapons development and formed alliances with typically authoritarian anticommunist leaders to spread the Gospels of Privatized Means of Production and Rule by Will of the People, so, too, does Henry desire to spread his essence through sex and procreation; the former led to more severe global environmental degradation and numerous genocides, the latter leads to sexual and emotional misery for all parties.

When Henry greets Mary at her house, their conversation is dampened by the scream of steam from an industrial heater in an adjacent apartment complex. Their dejection toward one another is both visible and verbal:

> HENRY: You never come around anymore.
>
> (*MARY X turns away from Henry for a moment, then opens the door.*)
>
> MARY X: Dinner's almost ready
>
> (*HENRY and MARY X enter the house.*)

Henry introduces himself to Mrs. X and sits on the couch with Mary next to Mrs. X's chair, and the three engage in stiff small talk over an ambient squeaking, revealed to be caused by a litter of puppies nursing from the family bitch. Mary then has an epileptic fit on the couch, and Mrs. X violently strokes her hair in attempts to calm her down. The primal acts of suckling teats and being menaced by a neurological illness are juxtaposed with the civilized act of idle conversation. The characters are apparently indifferent to the primal acts occurring in the background, but they are visibly uncomfortable at the civilized acts. Later, as Mrs. X is preparing the vegetables for a salad in the kitchen, an old woman sits in the corner corpse-stiff; Mrs. X uses the stiff woman as a ventriloquist dummy to toss the salad, places a cigarette in her mouth, then lights it. Being kept alive by her children against her will renders the old woman an inert husk—a puppet.

At dinner, Mr. X, the household patriarch, invites Henry to carve the chickens ("They're new—little damn things!") and as knife touches flesh the drumsticks twitch in unison and blood erupts from the rectum of the chicken, as if it were undergoing mammalian birth. This sends Mrs. X into a fit like Mary's, albeit more sexually charged; her eyes flick back into her head and her tongue moves as though it were giving cunnilingus. Despite sexual reproduction being natural and for most humans a *virtue* and a *duty*, the natal symbolism in this scene subverts the normalcy and purity of birth into an extreme grotesquerie, and it is grotesque because of the *utterly unnatural character* of these images.

A tearful Mary and Mrs. X storm out of the kitchen and into the other room, leaving Mr. X alone with Henry at the table:

MR. X: So, what do you know, Henry?

HENRY: Oh, I don't know much of anything.

Henry does not "know much of anything" in that he is allowing his sexual urges, emotional distress, and inability to live truly autonomously to pollute and ultimately overpower his "pure reason."

The light bulb in the living room burns out, and Mrs. X corners Henry in the foyer about his sexual relationship with Mary. Henry is reluctant to admit that he and Mary had sexual intercourse; he sees no reason why Mrs. X should be prying into such personal matters, but after Mrs. X insists she knows the truth Henry caves with a mere "sorry" with head hung. Henry's shame over having sex with Mary is telling about human attitudes towards sexuality: If the act of sex represents humans at their most intimate, then why does the flesh recoil like a firearm when it is pleasured; why do many people cringe with embarrassment when sex is brought up in conversation? Mrs. X reveals that Mary has given birth to a premature baby, and that Henry and Mary must wed to obtain proper custody. Still in tears, Mary asks Henry if he is opposed to the idea of marriage. Henry replies negatively and develops a nosebleed, like Pinocchio caught in a lie. As the light bulb burnt out before Mrs. X's talk with Henry about the child and his marriage to Mary, so does any hope of Henry redeeming his freedom and his happiness—the blood gushing from his nose represents the miscarriage of his soul.

Mary has moved into Henry's apartment with the baby, a grotesque, mewling creature, the head analogous to that of a horse fetus, limbless, swaddled, always referred to as "it." Mary wrestles with feeding the baby a spoonful of cereal, so she pinches its nostrils shut to get it down; or, by starving the child of oxygen, if only temporarily, Mary makes the child suffer solely to shut it up and to ease her maternal frustration.

On Henry's end, the pressure of fatherhood has disrupted his routine of sexual reverie by the radiator. Other personal needs are effectively neutered; the bed that he and Mary share is cold and chaste; their very wedding ring resembles a hookworm that Henry has stored in a cabinet. The baby cries at midnight and Mary leans down in the crib and shouts at it. Breaking down from lack of sleep, to Henry's dismay, she rips her luggage out from beneath the bed in a manner that resembles heavy sex or a doctor pulling a baby from a mother's uterus. Realizing Mary is not bluffing, Henry suddenly becomes indifferent to her departure.

Alone with the baby, Henry is more engaged with his parental obligation. He inserts a thermometer into its mouth, and when he withdraws it the mercury indicates a fever, and boils like those of the Man in the Planet spontaneously appear on the wheezing infant. Henry has an obvious yet profound epiphany: 'Oh, you *are* sick!" The enunciation in Henry's voice in this scene, and the spontaneity of the baby's leprosy, implies that Henry assumed conceiving a child would align with parental fantasies that children have when they play with dolls, and that the actual consequences of blindly reproducing have taken a sledgehammer to his mind. He places a boiling kettle close to the baby in the hopes of treating its fever and the mucous buildup in its lungs.

Henry and his baby are prisoners of each other. It refuses to let Henry abandon it stricken with illness; it reels him back in with its cries as he is about to step out the door. Likewise, Henry has imprisoned the baby in its crib, in linen swaddle, in existence itself.

When Henry goes to bed for the night, the film shifts to an iconic, surreal sequence in which a smiling blonde woman in a plain, white dirndl dress and with tumorous cheeks the size of melons shuffles from left to right on a burlesque soundstage inside Henry's radiator, to the accompaniment of eerie lounge music. As she dances, spermatozoa fall from the rafters and litter the stage. The woman squashes the dead gametes as they get in her way, never slacking in her smile.

The Lady in the Radiator is a personification of the Sexual Revolution: her white shoes are contraception; the white dirndl is the woman as the blank slate, free to pursue greater personal autonomy in a systemically patriarchal society; her monstrous cheeks represent a stronger sexual appetite enabled by the former; her beckoning smile is Henry's own sexual liberation, in that rather than being coerced into a practically asexual marriage in order to gain custody of an accidental child, Henry consents to a sexual and childless relationship in his dreams.

The Lady rushes back into the darkness after an agreeable performance, and Henry awakens to find Mary asleep next to him, smacking her lips and rubbing her eye obnoxiously and nearly forcing Henry off the edge of the bed. Henry reaches under the sheets and pulls ropes of sperm from his groin and throws them against the wall. The cabinet illuminates and its doors swing open. The hookworm wedding ring comes alive in a stop-motion animated sequence in which the ring flees to a lunar surface and slips in and out of the craters like a prairie dog, becoming subtly more massive in the meanwhile. So, Mary, in her absence, has been having extramarital affairs, and as the hookworm's mouth billows, gaping and black, so the stability of the marriage has become a void.

Henry is alone again. He assumes Mary has returned to the X household for the night. The Beautiful Girl Across the Hall visits Henry's flat and seduces him. Before the preliminary kiss Henry puts his hand over the baby's mouth to keep it from crying. They kiss passionately in a white pool like that from the opening. When the baby cries again, the Beautiful Girl looks at it with horror as Henry's lips are against hers. They symbolically drown in the pool.

In perhaps the most famous scenes of the film, The Lady in the Radiator returns, and sings in an androgynous voice:

> In Heaven, everything is fine
> You've got your good thing
> And I've got mine
>
> In Heaven, everything is fine

You've got your good thing
And you've got mine

In Heaven, everything is fine.

André Breton opens his foundational *Manifesto of Surrealism* with a maxim that resonates with Henry's emotional state at this point in the film:

> So strong is the belief in life, in what is so fragile in life—*real* life, I mean—that in the end this belief is lost.[3]

Love, happiness, and freedom are the fragile things in which Henry once believed, and in his disillusionment, he takes refuge in the delight of suicide.

When the Lady in the Radiator finishes her song, Henry approaches her on the soundstage. She receives him in her hands, and she glows violently. The Lady's illumination is interrupted by a shot of Henry's split-second hesitancy, and then concludes. The Lady vanishes, and the Man in the Planet takes her place. A wind blows the husks of sperm offstage. A rock crowned with two trees with intertwining branches rolls into frame, forcing Henry into a corner, where he spins a bar. Henry is decapitated by a phallus springing from his neck, and his head rolls on to the floor of the soundstage. The rock bleeds and floods the stage floor. The headless body of Henry continues to spin the bar as the shrieking head of the baby emerges from the neck. Henry's head falls into the pool of blood that came out of the rock and lands in a slum, where a boy brings Henry's head to a pencil factory. A portion of his skull is used to produce a batch of erasers.

---

[3] André Breton, *Manifestoes of Surrealism*, trans. Richard Seaver and Helen R. Lane (Ann Arbor: University of Michigan Press, 1972).

The trees recall the myth of Baucis and Philemon (Ovid, *Metamorphoses,* VIII 621-96), in which an old peasant couple are transformed into intertwining trees after showing hospitality to Zeus and Hermes in mortal disguise. As Baucis and Philemon were sentinels to a temple made from their former cottage, so are the man and woman in sexual union the sentinels of life and pain. Henry is ultimately inseparable from his child, and for every cry of pain, hunger, sadness, or anger that escapes the baby, Henry is ultimately responsible. When humanity, invested in Henry, recognizes the pain it has created through the seemingly innocent act of reproduction, and the species pledges abstinence, then utopian liberation that has even in the imagination can finally be achieved.

Henry awakens. There is a brick wall outside his window. In the streets below, Henry witnesses an assault next to a broken pipeline, its contents collecting in another pool. Mary is still gone. The sheets of his bed have been mutilated, as though moth-eaten. Desperate for companionship, he decides to visit The Beautiful Girl Across the Hall, but when he knocks on her apartment door she does not answer. He returns to his apartment and the baby laughs mockingly. Henry takes off his jacket and lies on his bed, then picks at his sheets. Suddenly he gets off the bed, puts his coat back on, and opens the door to find The Beautiful Girl caressing another man outside her door. She looks at him with faint disgust; from her vantage point Henry's head is replaced by that of the baby's. Henry sinks to the floor, utterly isolated. He contemplates the baby, takes a pair of scissors, and cuts through its swaddle, revealing its internal organs. Imprisoned in life, exposed in death. Henry stabs its heart and a foam volcano erupts from its body and engulfs it. Henry watches in horror. The baby's neck elongates, resembling its spermatozoon state. A short in the electrical outlet causes the lamp in Henry's apartment to stutter. A barrage of gigantic versions of the baby's face assault Henry's vision until the lightbulb kicks on. Henry watches the planet from the opening scene shatter. The lever in the Man in the Planet's domain sputters sparks, and it is ambiguous as to whether the Man is in bliss or in agony. Henry is transported to a vast white void, where he embraces the Lady in the Radiator.

The profanity of Henry's killing his baby is analogous to the profanity of Othello killing Desdemona: Despite both being driven to commit a paramount atrocity, the audience sympathizes with Othello, who has been deceived to the point of insanity by rumors of cuckoldry, just as they sympathize with Henry deceived to the point of insanity by the false prospects of life and fatherhood.

Henry is Lynch's Abraham; the baby is Isaac. But the Man in the Planet sends no angel to stop Henry from ridding humankind of pain; rather, his Angel in the Radiator embraces Henry's decision, for everything is fine in Heaven.

Bibliography

Breton, André. *Manifestoes of Surrealism*. Translated by Richard Seaver and Helen R. Lane. Ann Arbor: University of Michigan Press, 1972.

Olson, Greg. *David Lynch: Beautiful Dark*. Lanham, MD: Scarecrow Press, 2008.

Schopenhauer, Arthur. "On the Sufferings of the World." In *The Essays of Arthur Schopenhauer: Studies in Pessimism*. Translated by T. Bailey Saunders. Project Gutenberg, 2004. Accessed October 24, 2017. http://www.gutenberg.org/ebooks/10732.

Untitled
Artist: Dave Felton

The Theatre of Ovid

By Aaron Worth

17 May 1898
Constantza, Roumania

MY DEAR William,
When, a fortnight ago, I helped my new bride into the Parisian railway carriage that was to whisk us away on the first leg of our Continental honey-moon, I fancied that I would be too much occupied with the pleasures of the connubial condition to write many letters to London, even to such an old and true friend as yourself.

I could hardly have then foreseen, however, that her illness, which I had believed to be entirely in remission, if not vanquished altogether, could return so suddenly to plague us, without my having the least suspicion of it.

It is the old delusion, you see, though poured, as it were, into new bottles. She now imagines—

But I must not run ahead of myself. I forget that you do not know all the details of her case. Let me fill in the background first.

The many tongues of Rumour being as loquacious today as in the Bard's time, you will have heard, I suppose, that Charlotte was briefly a patient of mine, at Thornton House. If I have not spoken openly with you before upon this subject, it was not, believe me, from any lack of affection for you, or of regard for our friendship, but rather from a certain reticence not entirely unallied with feelings of—*shame*; I cannot in conscience call it by a gentler name.

To put it very bluntly: one hardly expects to find a wife in a mad-house, particularly one's *own* mad-house.

Moreover, despite the great advances our civilisation has made with regard to illnesses of the mind, no small degree of social *stigma* yet attaches, as you well know, to their sufferers. I have wished to spare Charlotte such embarrassment as I could.

So you may well believe that, if I broach the subject with you now, my dear friend, it is because I have very particular reasons for doing so.

I first met Charlotte in February of last year—then a girl of seventeen, and of remarkable beauty (as you have seen for yourself). I made her acquaintance, however, not in a drawing- or a ball-room, but in a well-padded cell. She was glaring at me, with a sullen and suspicious look which quite spoiled the effect of her lovely grey eyes.

The circumstances of her entry into my professional orbit were these.

She had possessed but a single relative in the world: an aged father (a classical scholar of some repute), with whom she had lived, near Oxford. Upon his death, Charlotte was left entirely alone, suffered a complete break-down of the nervous system, and was, shortly thereafter, admitted to my care.

The chief symptom of her condition was an extreme form of *grapho-mania*, i.e. an unnatural compulsion to write. The poor girl was found by a friend of the family, sitting, all alone, in the now deserted library of the house she had shared with her father. She was seated at his desk, bent over a very old and valuable edition of Sallust, in the margins of which she was scribbling. No, "scribbling" is unfair, as she was writing with great care, in a tiny yet precise hand. But the *matter* was the most utter nonsense. At first these rambling marginalia appeared to constitute an attempt at a scholarly essay, upon certain of the more obscure poetic *genres* practiced in antiquity. But they proved upon closer inspection to be a hopeless farrago of the most bizarre phantasies, in which were mixed some few fragments of accepted history, rather like raisins in a Christmas pudding.

It was subsequently discovered that fully half of her father's books had been defaced in the same fashion!

In those vandalised margins, wholesale invention mingled with accepted fact to produce an unnatural hybrid, the whole clothed in the sober language of scholarship, and supported by a myriad of fictitious authorities. (The style was, no doubt, an apelike imitation of her father's writing.)

She seemed to believe herself to be a kind of feminine Tacitus or Gibbon, charged with the task of writing a vast history (or ought I to say, *counter*-history?) of ancient times, though one, again, which was about ninety per cent rubbish in its composition.

A singular feature of her pathology, I should here mention, lay in her obsessive delineation of a host of wholly fictitious *institutions*—i.e. churches, cults, libraries, equestrian orders, secret societies, senatorial bodies, and the like, organizations having no historical existence whatever, except in her own fevered imagination.

As she had no guardian living, a period of compulsory treatment at Thornton was decided upon, as the best course of action.

When she was first admitted, and for some weeks to follow, the poor girl rebelled—nay, it is hardly an exaggeration to say *raved*—against her involuntary confinement (as is by no means unusual in such cases, as you well know). Daily she railed against her keepers, myself above all (her "chief gaoler," she called me! how it stabs me to the very heart now to think of it!).

But, in the months that followed, I helped her to see that her true prison was one of her own making. Its bars were not of iron, but of ink; with every chimerical bit of quasi-history Charlotte inscribed in the margins of her dead father's books, she immured herself more and more inescapably within a dungeon of delusion.

By slow stages, however, through long, patient talks—her slender, sylph-like hand in mine—I led her towards the light of sanity, until finally, the dear girl took the final step thither—quite of her own will, I rejoice to say.

This last step was, quite simply, fully and freely to *renounce* those mad, palimpsested volumes, and to consent to their destruction, which I am glad to say, she did without the least hesitation or equivocation. (The tomes in question had, in fact, already been consigned to the proverbial dust-heap long ago, on my orders; but the important thing was the mental *action* on her part.)

You will forgive me, I am sure, if I pass over in silence the period of transition during which an entirely professional relationship blossomed, most unexpectedly, into a courtship, complete with the most miraculous transformation of my own person, from mad-house doctor to husband!

Let it suffice to say, that the dear girl had developed strong feelings for me while under my care—feelings which were by no means unreciprocated.

What *is* important to the present account is some brief explanation of how bride and groom ended up in the backward waste-land of Roumania.

It began when I asked Charlotte where she would most wish to spend our honey-moon. The entire world, I declared with an histrionic flourish of my hand, was open to us. (This was perhaps a *little* disingenuous on my part, as I had dropped several broad hints in the weeks before our marriage, that I would greatly desire to see Wagner's *Parsifal* performed at Bayreuth.)

To my surprise, she mentioned the city of Constantza, in Roumania—which, she hastened to inform me (I am afraid I must have frowned), boasted a very picturesque setting, on the coast of the Black Sea.

When I asked her what in the world had put such a notion as that into her head, she looked timidly down at the carpet, and murmured something half-audible about the antiquarian attractions of the town, in particular some Roman remains she remembered her father speaking of once. But of course, she added quickly, looking up at me with earnest eyes, we should not go if I did not wish it, or if the distance rendered the journey impracticable.

At this I smiled and, taking her hands in mine, assured her that we should travel to Far Cathay, Timbuctoo, or the kingdom of Prester John himself, if it was her own heart's desire. The gratitude that shone then in her eyes was ample reward, as I thought, for my concession. (And besides, I realized, there was no earthly reason why we might not also stop in Bavaria upon our return home!)

After a seemingly endless journey, chiefly by rail, during which we seemed to leave modern civilisation further and further behind with each passing hour, we arrived at last in Constantza. It does, indeed, look upon the Black Sea; but I can say little else in its favour. I must say, I don't know why the Romans bothered about the place at all.

But Charlotte was much taken with it. Indeed, from the moment we stepped out of the archaic, smoke-grimed vehicle in which we terminated our journey she has seemed—how shall I put it? *Radiant*, that is the word I want.

At first this puzzled me very much. But in the six days we have been here I have, I believe, uncovered the reason for her excitement (which has bordered, at times, on the unseemly), and it is one, my dear Will, which gives me much pain.

To begin with (and it is not, believe me, any idle egotism which motivates the observation, but simple concern for my wife's mental well-being), Charlotte has not paid me a twopence's worth of attention since our arrival here. Instead, she is in a state of almost constant distraction. Wherever we go in the town and its wooded environs, she looks about her in all directions, an occasional murmur or cry escaping her lips, sometimes pulling out a tiny notebook and pencil to record some thought or observation. Two or three times I have gently asked her what she was writing, but each time she has put me off with some casual remark about the *beauty* of the place (sic!).

Once, very soon after our arrival at the hotel here, I thought I observed Charlotte to slip some object into one of the drawers of her dresser, in a suspicious manner. In light of the curious behaviour she has subsequently exhibited in our walks about town, I have felt myself quite justified in taking the liberty of examining her possessions (I waited, of course, until she was in the bath.)

I told you, Will, that Charlotte had won her freedom from confinement, and (as I had thought) her very sanity, by agreeing to the destruction of those classical texts which she had ruined with her mad annotations.

Imagine, then, my surprise and deep sorrow, when I pulled from beneath a neat stack of her under-garments a smallish volume of Ovid, whose margins were filled with her tiny, careful script.

My heart sank as I paged through the book (it is called *Tristia*—do you know it? I have only read the *Metamorphoses*, and that in Dryden's English translation). Nearly four-fifths of its pages had been defaced. She must, I reflected, have begun her sad back-sliding immediately upon her release from Thornton.

Muttering a curse, I dropped into an arm-chair and began to

read.

She had, I saw immediately, developed a new phantasy, though one quite consistent in general type with the others. She premises the existence of an ancient theatre, which—

But I shall let you read for yourself. Her "essay" begins thusly:

> Regarding the precise *circumstances* of the Theatre's foundation, there remain to this day legitimate grounds for dispute; but we may assign a *date* to its origins with something very like precision. The key lies in an (undoubtedly symbolical) episode related in the fourth book of the poet's last work, the *Epistulae ex Ponto*, composed in the sixth or seventh year of his exile, shortly before his death.
>
> After complaining for years about the barbarian population of remote Tomis (where he had been sent, by an implacable Emperor, for an unspecified "error," about which Mr. MacDonald has written what must be considered the most plausible account), Ovid now confesses to his friend and interlocutor that he has (as we should put it today) "gone native," becoming "almost a Getic bard" (*faciam paene poeta Getes*). He confesses that he has completed some new "work," marrying native and Roman elements.
>
> But what was this hybrid creation?
>
> The poet claims, of course, merely to have composed a conventional paean or encomium, in the Getic language, to the imperial family, forcing barbarian words, as with a shoe-horn, into Latin metres. Moreover, he would gull his readers into believing that he held a crowd of bellicose savages spell-bound with panegyrics to Augustus and Tiberius, their very quivers trembling in appreciation of his verse (*plenas omnes movere pharatras*)!
>
> This supremely improbable scenario has been incontrovertibly (and mercifully) exploded long ago, *as a literal account* (see Nathanson, Gabriels, Roushkoff).

But this imaginary episode, as Dr. Schütz has established beyond all rational doubt in his magisterial *Ovidstheater*, conceals, or rather enciphers, an important truth.

The poet did indeed develop a close *rapport* with the natives of Tomis during his last years and may even have learned to speak with them in their own language (though this is hardly the place to add fresh fuel to that particular *querelle*). But this was not, surely, to compose insipid hymns of praise to those who had wronged him. No: Ovid spent the anguished conclusion of his life in continuing, or ought one rather to say *completing*, his life's master-work, the peerless *Metamorphoses*.

Ah! But here we come to a highly fraught question (for some an essential question), namely:

Did the poet oversee the founding of the Theatre himself, as a place to stage his new tales of transformation? (It must be remembered, of course, that the people of Tomis were entirely illiterate.)

Or did he simply relate these in Homeric fashion to his rough auditors, who after his death began to enact them, as a means (initially at least) of preserving them?

I incline towards the latter theory, but do not insist upon it. We have had, surely, useless polemics enough in recent years over puzzles which are at the present time insoluble; if and when fresh evidence may come to light, students of the Theatre and its history will hardly be found behindhand in re-opening such questions!

In any event, however the Theatre came into being, we find that, in a relatively short time, it acquired something like fame. The young Claudius is said to have made a secret journey to Tomis in 21 or 22 AD, for the express purpose of witnessing for himself the performance of Ovid's unpublished transformations. If this is so, then it may well have been he who wrote the sadly fragmentary account of the Theatre (now in private hands), of which only the following words survive (the translation is Meyersault's):

> ... the Tragic stage (as we have always known it) being generally inhospitable to transmutation *as such*. This is not to say that change is never pictured by Aeschylus, Euripides, and the like masters of the old art, but only as it were by *accident*. On the other hand, in the Theatre of Ovid, transformation is acted almost entirely for its own sake; as an end in itself, to which all other elements (narrative above all) are wholly subordinated ...

Nor was this the only representative of the Julio-Claudian line to take an interest in the Theatre's productions. For it is surely one of history's crueler ironies that Tiberius, whose unremitting enmity had ensured the poet's death in exile, should, in the last year of his life, have summoned the Theatre—rather as if it were a pack of common strollers—to play for him at Capreae.

What transformation was acted upon this occasion is unknown, though the performance (as M. Renault has persuasively argued) was probably witnessed by the juvenile Gaius (or "Caligula," as he is known to history), upon whom it seems to have made a deep impression. The Emperor himself expired very shortly after this visit, though only a tiny minority of the Theatre's historians *openly* assert any connexion between the two events.

Such occasional peregrinations apart, however, the Theatre was not habitually or essentially peripatetic. Certainly it possessed a fixed *locus*, somewhere in or near the town whose soil held the poet's remains; i.e. an actual stage, with sophisticated apparatus for presenting miraculous and multifarious changes of bodily form; but precisely where this may have been is open to endless debate ...

Do you see it now, William? Or perhaps you have already guessed, before this? Here is the explanation for her strange behavior since we arrived here; nay, for her curious insistence that we travel to this wretched back-water in the first place, for our honey-moon! *For this is ancient Tomis*—something I might have surmised straightaway, had you and I pursued a classical education at "Oxbridge," rather than a practical one at Edinburgh! Yes, we are in the final resting-place of the Augustan poet, and poor Charlotte *is looking for her imaginary theatre*—searching the streets of Constantza for this phantom of her disordered mind, as if it were a real thing . . .

I do not even know, Will, whether I shall post these letters. For the moment, I am merely collecting them, between the pages of my day-book. Events, I suppose, will decide me: if our tale has a happy ending, I shall not, perhaps, feel the need to make these embarrassing disclosures to you. On the other hand, if it does *not*—

I do not like to think about it. But merely to write to you, Will, restores some of my equanimity of mind.

But I hear the gurgling of draining bath-water, from the next room. I must return the book to its hiding-place.

I shall write more later. My heart, dear Will, is quite broken . . .

18 May 1898
Constantza, Roumania

Dear William,

I have two deeply troubling developments to tell of—both springing, of course, from the same (sadly muddied) source.

The first, and most immediately alarming, is the fact that my wife, no longer content with making circumspect, diurnal investigations, appears to have begun searching *by night* for this chimera of her brain.

Let me tell you how I learned of this.

Very early this morning—three-forty-five, by my watch—I was awakened by the sound of our bed-room door opening (it creaks most damnably).

Blinking in confusion, I sat up in bed and listened intently as the door was slowly shut again—as stealthily and quietly as its ill-maintained hinges would allow.

I put out my hand for my wife, and finding that side of the bed quite empty, called out Charlotte's name in some surprise.

There was a silence of several seconds, and then came the sound of my wife's voice, timid and tremulous, from the darkness:

"John?" she said, seemingly much confused. "John, what am I doing out of bed, darling?"

I lit a candle (there seems to be no gas, much less electricity, to light this retrograde nation), fumblingly put on my glasses, and beheld poor Charlotte standing by the door, a coat thrown over her night-dress. Her eyes were wide and fearful, and her fingers plucked nervously at her throat.

"I must have been sleep-walking," she murmured, as I helped her to undress, "though I don't recall ever having done so before." A shiver shook her slender frame, as I put her to bed again. "Thank goodness you stopped me, dear, before I went any further than the door."

At this I frowned but said nothing, for besides the sounds I had heard, the testimony of her slippers and night-dress spoke loudly against such a transparent fiction, both being much coated with mud.

I cannot escape the conclusion that Charlotte was out for much of the night, God knows where, searching for a non-existent ruin—

and, what is worse, lying to me about it.

(She is sleeping now, as I write this, by candle-light.)

I should hardly approve such nocturnal perambulations in the heart of London—who knows what additional perils the girl courts by pursuing them in a foreign land?

Yet I hesitate openly to remonstrate with her as yet, as there is no telling what the shock of such a confrontation might do to her, in her current, fragile state of mind.

I should, however, like very much to be able to sedate her at night. Unfortunately, my medical bag, in which I carry some opiates, as well as a few surgical instruments, for emergencies, was stolen shortly after our arrival here (or did I already mention this?). I have made complaint at the desk downstairs, receiving only blank protestations of ignorance for my pains. (Probably the hotel's employés have had a hand in the theft—it is a nation of scoundrels.)

As regards monetary value, the loss is trifling, but under the circumstances it is damned inconvenient.

Well, I shall simply have to keep a closer eye upon her, especially at night.

The second development of which I spoke—

Wait a moment, Charlotte is stirring.

No, she sleeps still.

The other thing of which I have to tell, William, involves less perhaps of present danger, but is to me even more heart-breaking.

I speak, quite simply, of the progressive disintegration of her mental condition, as revealed in her delusional writings.

I have stolen every occasion I could to read further in the book she keeps hidden from me. I have it now, on the bed-table beside me (its author sleeping an uneasy sleep, at my other elbow!). I have waded through perhaps three-quarters of this morass of phantasy. With every page she writes (or rather, disfigures), Charlotte is drawn more deeply into her fixed idea, premised upon the existence of this imaginary play-house. And what is more disturbing to me, is the increasingly diseased *character* of the conceits and images she employs, in the elaboration of her pathetic "history." Her mind roils, I now perceive, with the most frightful scenarios of violence and horror, which she projects onto the imaginary stage of her "theatre."

But her own words are, surely, the most eloquent evidence of her state of mind:

> And now, with the later years of Antiquity, we enter upon that dark period of the Theatre's history, associated with its decadence and suppression.
>
> I should begin by saying, that I cannot myself accede to the theory, now becoming fashionable, that the Theatre, even at the very *nadir* of its degeneracy, ever became a mere play-house of horrors, like the *Grand-Guignol* theatre lately opened in Paris.
>
> Let me not be misunderstood. By this I mean simply to say, that it is inconceivable to me that some spark of the poet's original inspiration did not remain to animate even the debased productions of this period, with some measure of true artistry.
>
> For endless horrors *were* acted there, to be sure—horrors so shockingly conceived, and so vividly pictured (by means of cunning machinery which included a kind of primitive kinematograph or phantasmagoric projector), that an Empire which had winked at the depraved excesses of a Nero and a Commodus, now sent a picked detachment of Prætorians to the remote colony in secret, charged with the utter extirpation of the Theatre from the face of the earth, by whatever means necessary.

By way of example, my poor darling here relates—or rather fabricates—some five or six synopses of mythological stories (none of which is in the least familiar to me), supposed to have been performed by her imaginary theatre. (These are in a kind of "free verse," as I believe the term is, with the occasional lapse into iambic regularity.)

Each tale is positively redolent with horror; I cannot bring myself to summarize here even the least appalling of them. They are the most eloquent—and most depressing—indices yet, of the retrogressive state of her mental health.

After these dreadful abstracts, she returns again to her theme of the fictitious theatre's extermination:

> In this awful task the imperial powers succeeded, at least to all appearance: the Theatre was first driven underground (perhaps literally: see Halévy's essay, "Les Grottes d'Ovide"), before dying out altogether. (I do not count, of course, the feeble *simulacrum* of the Theatre which flourished for some years near Byzantium.)
>
> This apparent extinction proved, however, to be but a transitional phase in the Theatre's *own* transformation or metamorphosis; one analogous to the state of the *pupa* before its emergence, in transfigured glory, from the *chrysalis*.
>
> This period of rebirth, roughly coincident with the first stages of Western Europe's own Renascence, is characterized by a radical *erosion of distinctions*: the effacement, above all, of the dividing-line between Art and Life. In the Theatre, it became increasingly difficult to know, where *performance* ended, and *reality* began . . .
>
> Whereas the Theatre had previously been content to generate mere (if astonishing) illusions—*representing* transformation by means of paint, pasteboard, rope and pulley, as well as coloured lantern-light, cast upon skins—it now stamped its changes indelibly upon bodies, through a diversity of new devices and techniques.
>
> At the same time, there now appeared a decided attenuation, and ultimately *an utter dissolution*, of the boundary-line (the *membrane*, if I may so express it) separating player from spectator.

>   It becomes, indeed, a fair question to ask of the Theatre during this period: Had it an *audience* at all?
>
>   Were not all those who assembled beneath its roof in secret—those who stood, at the evening's commencement, upon the boards of the stage, as well as those who sprawled on the planks used as benches—equally subject to its laws? Were they not all, by the first light of dawn, equally likely to emerge from its doors in a transformed state, whether for good or ill?
>
>   Did not player and auditor now mingle their bodies without check or restraint—both together, and with the properties and implements of the Theatre—the better to effect more profound and irreversible changes?

There is much more, in the same vein.

Very obviously, a further period of confinement at Thornton House—probably a long one—will be necessary, upon our return to England. The roots of her illness are sunk more deeply than I had imagined. But the case is by no means hopeless. I have no doubt that with a more rigorous course of treatment she—

But she begins to stir, and murmurs my name, the poor darling. I must put the book away.

18 May (very late),
Constantza

When I wrote to you this morning, William, I spoke of the need to keep a close watch on Charlotte, for fear that, in her present condition, she might come to some harm.

My fears were, alas, too well justified: Charlotte's delusion has, this very night, led her into a highly dubious situation, to say the least.

Happily, my vigilance was rewarded, and I was able to lead her home without scathe either to body or honour. Furthermore, the worst of the crisis, I have reason to hope, may have passed . . .

But let me tell you what happened.

We went to bed, as has been our custom on this journey, at around nine o'clock. Bidding my wife good-night, I blew out the candle, and turned away, as if to sleep.

Then, after a quarter of an hour or so had passed, I counterfeited slumber by a very slow and regular breathing, while actually remaining wide awake, waiting to see if Charlotte would attempt another nocturnal expedition.

I had not long to wait. Not ten minutes after I had begun my feigned sleep, she slowly got out of bed and crossed to the door, frequently pausing as if to see if I stirred. Then I heard the creaking of the door, the sound of its closing again, and the soft patter of slippered feet scurrying away.

In an instant I was on my feet, struggling into my boots and jacket. I rushed from the room and hurried down the stairs and out of the hotel, where I looked wildly up and down the empty street. (My wife was much faster than I would have believed!)

Then I saw Charlotte, just vanishing into a doorway down the street, over which a wooden sign hung, in shape of a dragon.

I rushed to the spot, pushed open the door, and entered what proved to be a low, dingy tavern, in which some half-dozen grimy-faced men were drinking. Dully they stared at the strange foreigner who stood before them in striped pyjamas, panting and perspiring.

Ignoring them, I strode to the bartender (who wore a maddeningly knowing look on his wrinkled, seamed countenance), and demanded to know where my wife was.

At first, he affected not to understand English. Angrily I threw a few coins onto the bar, which he slid with a practiced paw into the filthy folds of his apron. Then, touching his drink-reddened nose, he bid me follow him into the back of that loathsome den.

After leading me through a dark tangle of malodorous rooms and hallways, he pointed to a darkened doorway, the shadow of a smirk on his lips. With a last glare in his direction, I hastened down a pitch-black flight of stone steps, finally emerging into a dimly-lit cellar of vast size.

There I found Charlotte, on all-fours upon on a packed floor of earth, in her night-dress!

In astonishment and disgust, I cried out her name, at which she turned her head in surprise.

In one hand, she held a rusty trowel, with which she was engaged in an *excavation* of the cellar's earthen floor! All around her pathetically quadrupedal form gaped wide and deep holes, ringed about with untidy mounds of earth, as though they were the handiwork of a host of monstrous moles.

Roughly I lifted her to her feet, seized her by one soil-stained hand, and without saying a single word more, dragged her from that place. As we passed the barman, he directed a most hateful leer at my wife, who I thought *winked* in reply; but in this I was surely misled by the uncertain light.

Neither Charlotte nor I spoke a single word, until we were back in our bed-room.

Once there, I ordered her to wash her hands, then began to pace the room angrily, giving voice to my profound disappointment in her conduct in terms rather more violent, perhaps, than I should have wished, had I been less irate.

I believe that an unthinking out-burst even escaped my lips of which the essence, if not the exact phrasing, was: *I ought to have left her in the mad-house* . . .

At this she broke down completely: falling into my arms and deluging me with tears.

She had been "wrong, utterly wrong": this was the import of her sobbing cries as she buried her face in my breast, a kind of wild joy infusing her words.

"John," she said at length, looking up into my face, her lovely grey eyes wet with tears, "Oh John, will it be at all to my credit if I tell you that I realise now, how *very mistaken* I have been?"

Soothingly I stroked her disordered hair and wiped her shining cheeks. She was not to blame, I told her. The phantoms of the brain could seem exquisitely real, to one in her condition.

I am not sure, however, whether she heard me. *All this time*, she began to murmur as I clasped the poor child to my bosom once more. *All this time* . . . Here I felt her shake again with a fit of sobbing (which for a moment—only a moment!—I took for *laughter*).

"We have all the time in the world before us yet," I whispered, rather lamely I fear.

Then, desiring that she should betake herself to bed straightaway, after her late adventure (once more do I feel the loss of those opiates, very keenly!) I suggested that she might take a glass of wine. (I have bought one or two of the local vintages, which are by no means to be despised.)

With a childlike shyness, she replied that *she* would take a glass if *I* would. I laughed and told her to fetch the bottle and two glasses from the sideboard. To your *health*, I said to her as I lifted my glass, laying particular emphasis on the last word, at which she crimsoned, most charmingly, and looked at the floor.

She sleeps now, there on the bed, as I write this. The poor child is, no doubt, quite exhausted, after all of these night-time rambles.

For that matter, I can hardly keep my *own* eyes open; it must be very late indeed . . .

Hum—I am rather surprised to see that it is not yet midnight; astonishingly, the events of tonight have taken less than two hours to unfold.

Yet I am *very* tired, of a sudden.

My eyelids droop; the room begins to swim.

Indeed, I find that I can hardly hold the

Earlier, I likened that chapter of the Theatre's history coeval with the Renascence, to the transformation of an insectile *pupa* into its final form.

But (as it was given me to understand a mere three days ago) I realise that a far more just comparison would have been with the *larval* stage of such a creature. For I can see quite clearly now (it is indeed as though my head were flooded with a luminous radiance, so powerfully do I perceive the truth!) that the Theatre was then entering, into not the *ultimate*, but the *penultimate* phase of its being. That such a final, and unspeakably glorious, transmutation *has now occurred*, however, it is no longer possible for me to doubt.

It was previously believed that, for those wishing to become initiated into the Theatre's secrets, entering thereby into its eternal fellowship, it was necessary to act a novel transformation upon the stage of the original Theatre.

But this is no longer the case.

This is because it no longer makes sense to speak of the Theatre as being contained within a single building or fettered to a particular locality . . .

Rather, *the Theatre must now be understood as a vast, invisible net-work, distributed across the surface of this planet, a net-work whose members may never behold one another in the flesh, though all are bound inextricably together by an intricate web of unseen filaments* . . .

That the Theatre should have evolved into such a form, is surely not to be wondered at, in an age in which wire-borne whispers slither and race beneath the very seas, penetrating into the remotest corners of the globe . . .

(A vivid and exact map of the net-work, with its profusion of connective points *clearly indicated,* may easily be perceived by the initiate.)

Henceforth, I now understand, initiation into the Theatre's sublime mysteries may be achieved by the simple expedient of *acting a transformation at any of the net-work's countless nodes or cruxes, and subsequently recording the new episode in the Theatre's eternal Archive, which has neither beginning nor end* . . .

Let the following, then, be officially entered into record within the Archive.

This transformation was acted upon 19 May, 1898, in Constantza, Roumania:

    The Rape of Clio

    Who does not know Clio, a Goddess born,
    Serene recorder of History?
    One day as she sat, among her books,
    A mortal dared interrupt her sacred labours.
    To another mortal was she taken
    In state of ignominious capture,
    And shut up in a prison, a dungeon of light.
    (Her books he gave unto the flames.)

    Here would he touch her, with his mortal hands
    And by other mortals suffer her to be touch'd.
    Here would he watch her, with his staring eyes
    And with droning tongue torment her sore
    With words, words, endless flow of words.
    But by a ruse she freed herself
    And brought her captor to a distant shore,
    Where 'twas ordained, her vengeance should unfold.

And now the hour of his reckoning has come.
First, she administers to him a sleeping-draught
Made from the juice of poppies crush'd.
Then, like a rainbow, she bends over his slumb'ring form
And touches him with fingers of silver,
Touches him in a thousand places,
Touches him all the night long,
While the knowing stars crawl in silence, far above.

At her Goddess-touch, shrivel away the fingers
That had filed her, one by one;
Then eyes and tongue fall away, ensanguined—
Ay, even those eyes that had stared and stared,
That tongue that would not be silent for an instant.
She touches too his loins, the seat of Priapus;
Then linger long her fingers at the place
Where Achilles' mother held her son

And lo! The rising cart of Phoebus
Now illumes a changéd thing.
What had been Man, has now become
One of the monstrous blind worms of the earth,
A mute and sexless creature.
Lamed and hobbled now, it can only crawl:
A being fit for tunnels, holes, and caves.
In dark earth shall it writhe and wawl—

But it stirs; it wakes.

The Alienation of the Self: Marx, Polanyi, and Ligottian Horror

By S. L. Edwards

Marx and the Puppet: Alienation

WRITING AS the industrial revolution marked its smoking path across the western world, Karl Marx remarked upon what he saw as the greatest horrors produced by capitalism and all its machinery. The system as it was then, pulled forward and apart by coal, steel, and morbidly squalid working and living conditions, separated human beings from their fundamental humanity. He wrote, "The *increase in value* of the world of things is directly proportional to the *decrease in value* of the human world."[1] In

---

[1] Karl Marx, "Alienated Labor," in *Writings of the Young Marx on Philosophy and Society*, ed. and trans. Lloyd D. Easton and Kurt H. Guddat (Garden City: Doubleday, 1967; reprint, Indianapolis: Hackett, 1997), 289 (emphases in original).

Marx's view, as the worker is set to produce more things, and as these things increase in value, the worker loses value as anything other than a manufacturer of products.[2] As the products themselves are mandated, rather than determined by workers' leisure or interests, workers are denied their fundamental creativity. Thus, they are bound to create things outside themselves, forced to birth unrecognizable and alien objects from their hands. Ultimately, Marx saw a labor force and a human race enslaved and ensnared by capitalism; what remained trapped in these chains was little more than a bipedal animal.[3]

Similarly, Thomas Ligotti offers his readers puppets. Featuring prominently in the various hollow shadowscapes of the Ligottian portrait of this world, the puppets represent an idea that echoes Marx's prophecy of alienation. The puppets, too wooden and too smooth to be human, are tied by their strings. The strings bind them not only to their controller, but to their fundamental nature *as* puppets. And the Ligottian protagonist (or perhaps *philosopher* is more appropriate) looks down on them and sees something horrific. The puppets are not horrifying simply because they are animated, haunted with life where there should be none. Nor are they speaking, a sort of tried and true strategy by which writers make their dolls haunted and alive to invoke a fear of the supernatural, a fear that keeps us out of rooms with too many dolls, lest they speak.

Rather, Ligottian fiction offers a very real fear of puppets in their fundamental reflection of what it means to be a human being: to be bound by strings and things. The puppet is a grotesque production of human effort, an all-too-successful attempt to understand mankind's lack of purpose against the bleak canvas of a wide universe where even the stars themselves are manipulated as

---

[2] Ibid., 290.

[3] Ibid., 292.

"bright puppets in the silent, staring void."[4] In this way, Ligotti adds to the horror invoked by Marx.

The worker is alienated from their production, and by extension from themselves. Marx writes that "the external nature of work for the worker appears in the fact that it is not his own but another person, that in work he does not belong to himself but to someone else."[5] This is particularly problematic for Marx, as labor is a fundamental part of human life and experience. He writes: "It [production and labor] is life begetting life. In the mode of life activity lies the entire character of a species, its species character; and free conscious activity is the species character of man."[6]

If producing something through one's own hands and mind is a fundamentally creative effort, then workers are denied their very creativity. They produce not only something they cannot recognize, but something they cannot own. Something they will *never* own. And because the laborer is an assumed person, defined by creativity, and the labor which they perform is not for themselves, they do not *own themselves*. And if they cannot perform their own labor, nor define their own products, then it is by no means an exaggeration that they *are not themselves*.

The laborer of Marxist thought, the product of the machine-world of the industrial revolution, may look down on the Ligottian puppet and see its strings. They may see its too-smooth features, its black and empty eyes. And because they have been denied their own humanity, we can venture that they might not see an alien product at all.

For this worker, the puppet is *an-all-too-real mirror*.

They look upon a pallid countenance, an idiotic smile, and see a

---

[4] Thomas Ligotti, "Dr. Locrian's Asylum," in *Songs of a Dead Dreamer* (New York: Carroll & Graf, 1989), 223.

[5] Marx, "Alienated Labor," 292.

[6] Ibid., 294.

grotesque, three-dimensional self-portrait. A laborer, forced to produce things alien to themselves, will inevitably produce the puppet. And rather than being unrecognizable, the production and realization of the puppet are the manifestation of an unwelcome truth: the non-existence of the self.

The self-delusion made manifest and physical.

Polanyi, Ligotti, and the Town: The Satanic Mill

Karl Polanyi, writing in 1944 amidst the final days of WWII, in turn echoes Marx. His previous homes of Budapest, Vienna, and London had been burned and scarred by the war, one that he saw stemming from a single, particular phenomenon. For him, both fascism and the radical communism of the USSR were part of a "double-movement"—an attempt by governments to unfetter their markets while society drew away from them.[7]

Like Marx before him, Polanyi saw capitalism as containing contradictions which would ultimately be its undoing. However, rather than revolution, Polanyi's proposal is more modest, though no less complicated: simply place the rules of the market back under those of society; simply dispel the myth that markets had ever been separate from society.

Famously, Polanyi asked a rhetorical question that begins his inquiry into the nature and history of markets as separate from society: "What 'satanic mill' ground men into masses?"[8] His sweeping history of the Industrial Revolution and the preceding centuries outlines the slow, methodical process through which laws and society were changed to accommodate a new ideology of global

---

[7] Karl Polanyi, *The Great Transformation: The Political and Economic Origins of Our Time* (Boston: Beacon Press, 2001 [1944]), 67-68.

[8] Ibid., 35.

economy. The result was the rise of poverty, pauperism, devastation of the countryside, and migration from it.[9]

As for Ligotti, the fictional corporations that plays a central role in some of his stories do not seem to fit the mold of an evil, clandestine organization. Indeed, they often produce absurdly and horrifyingly nonsensical products, in which lie their horrors. Likewise, Ligottian fiction presents to readers not the corporation itself but its ghosts. Abandoned towns. Industrial parks. The wreckage of globalism that has left Detroit a mausoleum of American manufacturing.

Polanyi would say the pendulum of unfettered global markets swept like a scythe across these places. And, indeed, it seems hard to argue against this. The graveyards made by corporations pockmark the Ligottian world, highlighting the temporary nature of mankind's endeavors.

The Ligottian would add, however, that such transformation exposes not only a contradiction, but a futility. And this futility is not only placed upon capitalism. Indeed, all human activity and industry are conclusively useless.

The narrator of "The Small People," for example, notices this in the machinations of the puppet-people who build their plastic, miniature town. Their buildings are wobbly, their foundations weak. There is simply no way that a town, be it of plastic or brick, can withstand the forces of time. The seeming awareness of the futility of their actions gives the "smalls" more genuineness than their human counterparts.[10]

For Polanyi, unfettered markets were an engine of destruction, things to be recoiled from. The Ligottian would agree, but, as with Marx, would add a horror onto this conclusion: The "satanic mill"

---

[9] Ibid., 35.

[10] Thomas Ligotti, "The Small People," in *The Spectral Link* (Burton: Subterranean Press, 2014).

is not only a part of markets, but of towns and communities as well. And rather than grinding men into masses, rather than reducing them to paupers, it reduces them to the truth. The meaninglessness of activity only produces monuments to mankind's fear of a greater void: Towers and factories are only ineffective bulwarks against the blackness and wideness of the sky.

Unfettered markets are certainly one engine of destruction, mechanisms that have accelerated destruction. But they are not the *only* satanic mills. These mills are woven into the very fabric of towns themselves, the lies of fictional communities and absurd corporations.

And they do not grind men into masses, because a mass is as inconsequential as an individual. Rather, they simply grind mankind down into its truer nature: the keepers of its own expansive crypt.

Ligottian Clarity: A Theme of Great Lies

The place where Marx and Polanyi would diverge from Ligotti lies in the core of his fictional and nonfictional conceptions of reality: nobody is anybody. You are not your head. There is a conspiracy against the human race, a myth of meaning that serves to perpetuate the species' existence against the truth of meaninglessness. Only the demoralized can successfully acknowledge the truth; anything less is a cowardly lie.

Even in his grimmest writings, Marx offers a more optimistic tenor: Workers, so successfully ensnared by capitalist chains, only need break them. Polanyi, for his part, believes the ever-swinging pendulum of the double-movement can be escaped if the lie of disembedded markets is exposed and acknowledged. The forces of capitalism can be subsumed and overtaken by social forces: our priorities need only be realized.

For the Ligottian, for the thoroughly demoralized, this does not matter. The truth of existence is that there is no reason for it. No justification.

This is not to confine the Ligottian to a corner of inaction, or to place the Ligottian philosophy outside of, or deem it irrelevant to, politics. Rather, it adds a layer of horror to the author's and reader's interpretation of reality. One might be aware of this truth and still go through daily motions, still try to make the world better or more tolerable.

But there is no utopia. There is only our bright-puppet planet being pulled through the stars by unyielding strings, and to fight against these strings is futile and cosmically juvenile.

Significantly, both Marx and Polanyi agree that there are great lies in place against humanity. Marx writes that "theology explains the origin of evil by the fall of man. That is, it asserts as a fact in the form of history that it should explain."[11] In the same manner, capitalism explains itself as emerging from a primordial, fictitious state of nature. Mankind is made to believe that this simply *is*, and that it has simply *always been*.

Likewise, Polanyi explains that perceptions of reality were completely rewritten to accommodate the brutal laws capitalism demanded. Poignantly, he writes, "Man was forced to resign himself to secular perdition: he was doomed either to stop the procreation of his race or to condemn himself wittingly to liquidation through war and pestilence, hunger and vice."[12] In order to explain the presence of extreme poverty alongside economic success, the desires of the individual and community were inexplicably connected. To explain a failure, one must tie it to the success of a greater society: "[T]he individual should respect economic law, even if it happened to destroy him."[13]

Marx and Polanyi both posit that explanations for reality,

---

[11] Karl Marx, "Alienated Labor," 289.

[12] Polanyi, *The Great Transformation*, 88.

[13] Ibid., 89.

whether they be religions or laws of economics, were created on fickle and contradictory ground. The failure of mankind explains history, but there is no offered history of mankind that is not contingent on this explanation. *Why* has it failed? *Because it simply has.* Why does one starve while, two neighborhoods over, houses throw away the food they cannot be bothered to eat before it goes bad? Because this is *economic reality* carefully constructed over the course of centuries.

The Ligottian philosopher-protagonist of "The Small People" asks an asylum doctor how we could possibly know if some great, reality-altering conspiracy was taking place: "Because we [mankind] have done it before."[14]

To explain away things—things that ultimately undermine any lie of meaning—great lies and contrivances may be created and proliferated through a variety of doctrines and scholastic circles. This a central, recurring theme of Ligottian horror, that perceptions of reality are fictitious, misguided, and ultimately *delusional*.

Though for the Marxist chains can be cast off, and for Polanyi markets can be subdued, this is not the case in a Ligottian world. For the Ligottian, the strings will never be removed. The vision of a better world is simply that, a *vision*. The better world is a dream, an apparition, and is just as illusory as any other reality.

What remains is to be pulled along by our strings. And as much as Marx might suggest we cast them off, or Polanyi that we take their rein, the Ligottian suggests that this, and indeed all of existence, is merely a contrivance.

---

[14] Ligotti, "The Small People," 58.

Bibliography

Ligotti, Thomas. "Dr. Locrian's Asylum." In *Songs of a Dead Dreamer*. New York: Carroll & Graf, 1989.

———. "The Small People." In *The Spectral Link*. Burton: Subterranean Press, 2014.

Marx, Karl. "Alienated Labor." In *Writings of the Young Marx on Philosophy and Society*. Edited and translated by Lloyd D. Easton and Kurt H. Guddat, 287-300. Garden City: Doubleday, 1967. Reprint, Indianapolis: Hackett, 1997.

Polyani, Karl. "The Self-Regulating Market and the Fictitious Commodities: Labor, Land, and Money." In *The Great Transformation: The Political and Economic Origins of Our Time*. Boston: Beacon Press, 2001.

Strange Bird

By Ian Mullins

The gale picks through
yesterday's bones
like an elephant sorting
ivory. Here a pigeon,
there a sparrow. Perhaps
a human finger.
A daily cull scraped
from skin then deposited
here, in a timid corner of
crumbled wall.

But in a thousand years
or less
an inhuman hand
will sort the centuries' debris
and wonder at this
strange assembly of worry
and wart. All bones present and correct; but how
did this bird

ever take to the air?

Solar Flare

By Paul L. Bates

MY FRIENDS *are not my friends.*
He repeated the phrase over and over like a mantra, driving the dark and deserted road doing his utmost to ignore the unsettling effect the fading streetlights had upon the oily darkness. His headlights weren't any better. If he trusted his eyes, the pavement immediately in front of the car was awash with a viscous layer that glowed a pale and sickly green where the beams crossed, as if something unnatural had just rained down from the clouds, had coated the blacktop with something utterly unwholesome. But he knew it had not rained. There was nothing on his windshield.

My friends were never my friends, he changed the wording.

How could these fragile friendships have become so totally illuminated by this sudden darkness? he added, breaking the rhythm.

He felt a need for speed, exercised caution instead. As much as he wanted to be quit of this place, have done with the whole business, he would not risk an accident. The ooze covering the street gradually thickened, like cement drying; it clung to his tires, a malevolent volition making itself known by doing its utmost to hold him fast.

He repeated the new variation of the chant, avoided thinking about why he ventured into the night against his comforting proclivities, why he had accepted the insidious invitation against his best judgment. *It must end*, he reminded himself. *One way or another it will end tonight. One way or the other I will finish it.* He accelerated just enough to compensate for the road's intractable resistance.

The decaying structures that lined the shabby main street, depressing during the best of times, had faded while he drove, faded at last from the merest suggestions of light washing across their windows to formless smears, neglected shadows cowering against the greater shadow of the night, no longer subject to the effects of the streetlights or the laws of nature as he understood them.

It was too soon to be looking for street numbers, he knew, but still he wondered how under these conditions he could possibly know the place.

My friends are automatons; their actions are all preprogrammed.

He drove for several more blocks, or what he thought were blocks. The only clue was streetlights bunched together at likely intersections, one on every corner in lieu of traffic signals, he assumed. *Why the hell did they pick a dump like this?* Eventually the engine complained, the car slowed, red and amber warning lights in the dashboard flickered, then faded. He pulled to the side of the street, hoping nothing was parked there, as he could see only the dim lights above him and the shrinking black slick on which he drove.

To his surprise, his shoes did not stick to the pavement. Outside the car, his visibility improved, if only slightly. He found a flashlight in the glove box, took it with him. He shined it on the nearest storefront where it illuminated a swirl of something like fine dust that obscured whatever lay behind it. Cautiously, he climbed the curb he knew must be there, groped the air for obstacles, wondered why he wasn't choking on whatever fluttered in the light beam. Step by cautious step he approached what he hoped would be a building until his hand felt something moist, cold, throbbing like a frightened animal. He jumped back, swung the flashlight like a weapon, all the while hoping to see a number rending the infernal darkness, willing to accept the likeness of anything recognizable, seeing nothing whatever by its feeble light save the endless swirling specks he could not otherwise sense against a blackness deeper than he thought possible. Turning around he shined his light back toward his car, but it might as well have been parked miles away.

At that awful moment, when even the mantras failed him, he heard a sound. At first he thought it was music, but it was too steady, too arrhythmic. He turned slowly in a circle, using his ears as he might have used his eyes. After an initial disorientation that terrified him more than the almost tangible darkness, he decided the noise originated further down the street. Taking only the smallest steps he approached the crackling sound, which grew no louder. He paused again, canting his head from side to side until he decided the sound emanated from his right.

Once again he approached what he assumed to be a continuous wall of storefronts. He touched something firm, not wood nor glass, neither stone nor metal. When he rapped on it with the edge of his fist, the noise stopped. He heard the sigh of a door opening, saw the swirling particles sucked into an even darker void, felt himself drawn along with them. The door shut of its own accord with a soft thud behind him, like a body in a sack landing on the pavement. Here he could taste the air. It was dry, stale, as if the dust of ages had irrevocably settled upon this place. His footfalls rustled, as if he were walking on loose sheets of paper.

The crackling began anew, from still deeper within, but his flashlight no longer illuminated anything. He shut it off, pushed it into his overcoat pocket. Refusing to budge, he listened to his sluggish heartbeat, his now labored breath, the steady noise beyond.

After what felt like an eternity, a vertical line of the palest light penetrated the gloom, but at what distance he could not judge. It widened until he recognized it as another door opening, as if whoever held the knob was rethinking their action even while performing it. The noise grew louder.

"He should be here by now," someone muttered.

He recognized Trisha's voice, but not her tone, cautious, fearful, resigned. He opened his mouth to speak her name, thought better of it, watched the band of pale light shrinking, disappear altogether, not so much as a streak left beneath the door. His instincts told him to run, to get as far away from this madness as possible.

Run where? he admonished himself. *It's all disintegrating.*

He walked as fast as he dared toward where he guessed he had seen the light, hoping no obstacles would intervene, the rustling sound following him like a dog.

I came to end it. I can't end it by running. I can't let it end itself.

He found the wall, or what he hoped was a wall. It was anything but smooth, even coarsely hairy in places, cold and clammy to the touch, the dry air notwithstanding. He tasted the bile rising to his mouth.

My friends are not my friends. My friends are not my friends. My friends were never my friends. My friends were never my friends.

Working his way down the wall, he found a protrusion, not a doorknob exactly, nor even a lever handle. It felt uninvitingly limp, like a small bloated bladder, filled with something cool, liquid, yielding. At his touch the door opened as before. He pushed it inward, hurried after it, his heartbeat accelerating.

Someone flung themselves at him, their arms loose around his neck.

"You came," Trisha said, her whispered voice racing like his heart. "I'm so glad."

She pecked him on the cheek, pulled away as if the contact were painful before he could respond in kind, her footfalls as silent as the night. He saw only the silhouette of a smallish woman, lithe and fearful like a deer, vanishing silently past occasional glimmerings into the shadows beyond.

He listened for more footsteps, but they were lost against that other sound, steadily grinding away until he thought he would go mad. Then the static stopped again, and someone cursed beneath their breath.

Here and there he noticed cones of light, little more than suggestions really, and always speckled by whatever gave the stale air its lasting flavor of decay. Within these gossamer cones black lumps waited, some jostling one another accidentally, as if dying spotlights shined their last on living shadows huddled beneath them.

I must make one circuit, he decided, *one last circuit before they're gone. Say my goodbyes. End it once and for all.*

He never realized how heavy his feet could be, how inconveniently gravity could play its only trick, holding him fast like familial ties. He trudged to the nearest pool of glimmering dust. He noticed it was only his footfalls that rustled.

He paused before the nearest cone of hovering dust and shadow. The crackling noise began anew, louder than before.

"What are you doing?" he demanded of the smallish mound of black before him.

"Trying to get the news," Bradford growled. "Want to get the latest on the solar flare."

He nodded his understanding knowing it nowise mattered. For a moment, he seriously considered taking full advantage of the situation, of kicking Bradford with all his might, but the effort required was beyond him. The static droned on and on while the hunched shadow quivered with anticipation, rose ominously, merged with another shadow he had not noticed before—possibly Rosa. He was suddenly thankful Bradford had nothing left to say.

Backing away he shuffled blindly, occasionally bumping objects he could neither see nor identify, by turns immobile and yielding, each a surprise, each with its own distinct and lasting pain. At the next shimmering pool of dust, two black mounds loomed above him, twin peaks of unending darkness.

"Do come closer," Matilda said.

She was standing on something, he realized, a table, a ladder, a platform—something to give her unwarranted stature in the darkness. Matilda's sister tittered foolishly beside her.

"Watch you don't fall off," he advised them, backing away. He would gladly have knocked their perch out from under them if he could have seen it, known it for what it was.

Small arms wrapped themselves about his neck again. He felt Trisha's lithe body press against him. "So glad you could make it," she whispered in his ear. Another peck on the cheek and she was off again, soundlessly flitting past the pale cones of light as if she were galloping away from a hungry predator.

He recognized Norbert by his puckered lips, his flabby cheeks, the ridiculous shank of hair that refused all ministrations of a comb—a face, he remembered, like the ass end of some bloated hybrid mammalian slug. Even as a shadow, Norbert stood out. A dozen appropriate insults flitted through his mind. Not one found its way to his tongue. They stood beyond one another's reach, Norbert huddled safely within his cone of shimmering dust, he within night's endless embrace, their lengthy expressions of mutual loathing and disgust lost against the bleak ambience of the ruin.

"Over here," a lilting voice drew his attention from the next cone—Giselle. "Let me tell you of my immediate needs."

That's enough, he decided. *This is getting me nowhere.*

He knelt, dug until he found matches in his coat pocket. Sweeping the floor with his hands he gathered the layer of brittle newsprint on which he shuffled, clutched the individual sheets, balling them, arranging them in a mound. The persistent static veiled the sound of his intentions.

He struck a match, held it to the closest wad of faded paper, but it burned only his fingers. He flung it away, struck another match, picked another spot for his conflagration, but the uncooperative newspaper remained steadfastly fireproof. After the third try he gave up.

It took a humiliating eternity of labored shuffling before he found the first door, the one with the clammy bladder for a handle; another equally humbling eternity to find the second. The taste of decay slowly abating beyond the interior.

Night was absolute without, even the pale glow of the streetlights no longer mocked his pitiful attempts at progress. His flashlight was useless as well. He blinked into its pristine glare to satisfy himself it worked at all, but the beam obstinately refused to locate his car. What could mere headlights do against this irresistible onslaught of the void were he to find the car anyway? Where would he go now that everything had willingly merged into the eternal night?

He stood alone on the sidewalk, the tepid air coagulating steadily around and within him, listening to the steady sound of that distant static, proof of the predicted solar flare, oddly comforting until it, too, was gone.

Night Walks: The Films of Val Lewton

By Michael Penkas

"I like the dark. It's friendly."

— Irena Dubrovna, *Cat People* (1942)

IN 1942, RKO Pictures set up a horror film division intended to compete with the very successful Universal monster movie franchises. After losing a fortune on the commercially disastrous (but artistically brilliant) films of Orson Welles, RKO couldn't match the budget of Universal and didn't trust its producers to act without studio oversight. When they hired producer Val Lewton (whose only production credits were second unit work for David O. Selznick at MGM), they placed a number of restrictions on him. The two restrictions that did the most to define Lewton's unique batch of horror films were that each film had to be produced for less than $150,000.00 and each film would have a title supplied by the studio.

The budget limitations (about one-tenth of what was spent to make a Universal horror film) meant that Lewton had no hope of producing an over-the-top monster bash like *The Wolf Man*, *The Ghost of Frankenstein*, or *The Mummy's Tomb*. However, rather than being a weakness, the low budgets forced him to use shadows and dialogue to suggest something far more sinister than the Universal monsters.

The titles supplied by RKO, like *Cat People* and *I Walked with a Zombie*, suggested monsters and special effects that Lewton could never afford on the budget provided. But he would clear this hurdle as well, using the titles as springboards for films that surprised the viewers by giving them so much more than what they were promised.

One of the most effective techniques used by Lewton in his films was the night walk. Every one of his horror films employs some variation on this simple, but very effective, method of generating suspense. Someone (often a woman) is walking along a dark path (a street, a dirt road, a hallway). This woman is usually alone (in either a literal or emotional sense). The scene is normally presented without music, relying instead on the natural sounds around her. Slowly, she becomes aware that she is not alone. Strange sounds begin to mingle with the natural ones. The woman begins to move more quickly, trying to escape an unseen horror. The scene ends in one of two ways: some loud noise breaks the tension and returns the woman to a relatively safe experience . . . or the darkness catches her.

The effect has been done many times in horror films that have followed Lewton's 1940s masterpieces. It is an effect that likely predated his work, but no one did more to define this film trope than Val Lewton.

Over the course of nine horror films (and those later produced by his immediate successors), the night walk evolved from a simple tool in the filmmaker's kit to a commentary on something far more haunting, something that scared audiences because it revealed a horror that was never confined solely to the screen, a horror they brought with them into darkened theaters around the world. Although probably nobody who saw a Val Lewton film ever had to cope with a shapeshifting panther, zombie, or Satanic cult, every one of them took the occasional night walk.

Cat People (1942)

The first Lewton-produced horror film, *Cat People*, premiered in late 1942 and garnered both commercial success and critical praise. The story concerns Irena Dubrovna, a Serbian immigrant and fashion designer, and Oliver Reed, a marine engineer, who meet, fall in love, and get married. The conflict begins when Irena reveals that she believes she is descended from Mameluks, a race of witches who would turn into vicious panthers when excited by rage or lust. The practical result of this belief is that Irena is unwilling to consummate her marriage to Oliver (or even so much as kiss him), which drives him to seek comfort in the arms of his co-worker, Alice Moore. At one point in the film, Irena follows the couple, remaining out of sight as they enjoy a quiet meal together. When Alice and Oliver part ways, Irena follows Alice, and our first night walk begins.

The only sound that can be heard at first is the shotgun-loud clicks of Irena's heels as she stalks behind Alice, hidden by the shadows between streetlights. The camera stays on Alice as the heel clicks following her suddenly stop. Has Irena turned off the sidewalk and given up the chase? Or has she become a creature whose footfalls are silent? The answer is never explicitly given, but

Alice begins to suspect that someone is following her. She looks behind her shoulder several times, and now Alice's heel clicks can be heard as she moves with increasing speed, trying to outrun something that cannot be seen. The heel clicks are now coming as rapidly as Alice's heartbeat, when suddenly there is a horrible scream . . .

Of a bus pulling up. Alice, visibly shaken by her experience, quickly steps onto the bus. There are some rustling trees, followed by a scene change to the interior of the zoo, where several sheep have been killed and muddy paw prints abruptly change to high-heeled shoe prints that end at Irena, composing herself and wiping something from her lips.

The whole scene lasts less than three minutes, but it changes the direction of the rest of the film. Until this point, the suspense is based on the question of whether or not Irena is mad and might do herself harm. After this scene, the soft-spoken and quirky woman is revealed as a threat to everyone else in the film. This scene would have been infinitely weaker with a stock horror movie soundtrack or a woman in a panther mask being shown on screen. Since the panther is never shown, it is never known where it is lurking. The shadows not only keep the danger hidden; they also make it omnipresent.

I Walked with a Zombie (1943)

After the theatrical success of *Cat People*, Val Lewton was relatively secure to continue producing these subtle horror films for RKO, but the $150,000 cap and studio-selected titles remained. It is hard to imagine anything subtle being produced under the title *I Walked with a Zombie*, but Lewton proved that he was more than equal to the task.

The plot—which is often compared to that of *Jane Eyre*—concerns Betsy Connell, a Canadian nurse hired to care for a woman on the Caribbean island of St. Sebastian. The woman, Jessica Holland, has suffered a spinal injury, which has erased her personality but left her still able to move and obey any command she is given. While caring for Jessica, Betsy engineers several attempts to revive her, eventually seeking the aid of the voodoo practitioners who live on the island. Thus, Betsy and Jessica make their way through a sugar cane field for a truly nightmarish night walk.

While Betsy is not physically alone, Jessica is no true companion. She does not speak and can do nothing to help. Betsy could be murdered beside Jessica without eliciting so much as a change in the latter's expression.

Furthermore, while a ghostly whistle can be heard accompanying the two women, it is quickly revealed that the sound is merely the wind blowing through a hollowed-out gourd and (rather ominously) an animal skull. They pass bone sculptures and hanging corpses before reaching the crossroads and meeting the wide-eyed zombie guardian, Carre-Four. The whistling bone-winds are slowly replaced by drumbeats as the three of them move toward the source of horror, instead of away from it. The complete lack of dialogue throughout this journey reinforces the sense of solitude. Despite her two companions, Betsy is alone on her night walk, heading towards a darkness she does not understand.

This will not be the last time a night walk occurs in the company of others, where it is made clear that loneliness is more than a physical state.

The Leopard Man (1943)

Based on the novel *Black Alibi* by Cornell Woolrich, *The Leopard Man* is one of the earliest serial killer films (although that term is never used, since it had not yet been coined). The story opens with Jerry Manning presenting his business partner, Kiki, with a trained leopard for her to use in her nightclub act. Kiki's rival, Clo-Clo, scares the leopard, leading to its escape. A series of murders follow, all attributed to the animal, but Jerry begins to suspect that a human killer is at work, using the escaped leopard as a cover for his own murder spree. This film boasts four night walks, one for each of the three victims plus a final one for the killer.

The first night walk follows a young woman, Marta Delgado, as she goes in search of corn meal. The leopard has just escaped, and she knows that it must be somewhere near. Some earlier dialogue with the leopard's trainer (the "Leopard Man" of the title) indicates that the animal might be scared into attacking if it hears a loud noise. Marta's night walk quickly takes her past the familiar streets, where the shops are already closed for the night, and into a quiet wasteland. At one point, she passes beneath a shadow-filled overpass, literally taking her to the "wrong side of the tracks," where she acquires the corn meal. On her way back, the walk beneath the tracks is stretched out as she starts at every shadow, before the tension is finally broken by a train rumbling overhead. However, unlike the bus in *Cat People*, the loud noise signals doom rather than salvation, as it scares the leopard, causing it to attack.

The second night walk is a far more abbreviated affair, as Consuelo visits a cemetery, both to leave flowers on her father's grave and to meet her lover. As she waits, the caretaker locks up the cemetery gate (symbolically joining her with the dead). Consuelo's brief night walk between grave markers is interrupted by the sound of a nearby car starting up on the other side of the cemetery wall. Her screams catch the driver's attention, and he promises to find a ladder and return for her. Here is another false reassurance at the end of a night walk. The stranger on the other side of the wall has assured Consuelo that she is not alone and will be delivered from death, but his help will come too late for her, as some unseen predator climbs the wall before his return and ends her life.

The third night walk follows Clo-Clo. It begins with a fortune-teller doing a three-card reading that indicates money, something black, and then death. The reading is repeated, with the same result. Clo-Clo has received some money from a generous patron earlier in the evening, and her night walk home has us waiting for something dark. When a wealthy man in a black car pulls up to Clo-Clo and begins a conversation, she realizes that he is part of the doom foretold, and she runs from him. Clo-Clo arrives home and it seems that she has averted her fate, but it is a false end to the night walk, as she discovers that she has dropped the money she received from the club and must go back out into the night. All signs show that she will not survive a second temptation of fate, and when she at first mistakes her killer for her boyfriend, it becomes clear that a leopard is not to blame.

The final night walk is Mr. Galbraith, a museum curator who has been acting as a sounding board for Jerry's theories throughout the film. The walk begins as he passes the cemetery where Consuelo died and hears her calling to him for help. It continues down the alley where Clo-Clo died, where a cigarette butt seems to fall from nowhere. He returns to his museum, only to be haunted by the sound of Clo-Clo's castanets. Eventually, he realizes that his night walk was staged by Jerry and Kiki, who suspect him of the murders. The film ends with a religious procession in which everyone in the town participates in a night walk of sorts. Galbraith tries to lose himself in this crowd, but he is easy to distinguish from the robed figures and is captured. He admits that he killed the leopard a week ago, but told no one, using it as a cover for his own murders. The gunshot that ends his life is another variation on the loud shock that ends a night walk.

The Seventh Victim (1943)

Although its plotline centers on a Satanic cult, *The Seventh Victim* lacks any supernatural element or even the ambiguous possibility of the supernatural, being instead a solid example of film noir. The story concerns Mary Gibson's search for her sister, Jacqueline. As Mary's search draws the attention of the cult to which Jacqueline belongs, the lives of everyone who gets near to either of these women come in danger. This film has two very different night walks.

The first night walk occurs early in the film. A private investigator, Irving August, helps Mary break into Jacqueline's former business. August has already checked out the business under false pretenses during the day and was given access to every room except one. Under cover of darkness, the two of them break in to investigate that one room. Of course, the mystery room is at the end of an unlit hallway. Up to this point, Mary has presented herself as an innocent, spiritually pure individual whose only interest is finding her missing sister. It is genuinely chilling to watch this soft-voiced young woman manipulate Mr. August into walking down the dark corridor to investigate the room alone. His walk is punctuated by a ticking clock, giving every impression of a condemned man walking to his death. Mary simply stands and watches him go, driven to find her sister, but not so brave that she won't send another into danger in her stead. When Irving August returns, he remains silent, saying nothing of what he saw. At first his silence seems to indicate shock, but then he stumbles, clutching his side, and Mary sees that he's been stabbed. Mary runs from the dead man, never even considering taking the same night walk that led to his death.

Eventually, Jacqueline reveals that she was being held by the Palladists, a Satanic society. As Jacqueline walks through the busy streets of Greenwich Village, she grows aware of a man following her. Her night walk is largely silent, and, though she is surrounded by passersby, she is still very much alone, as each person she turns to for help walks past her, not wishing to get involved. Whatever the man pursuing her intended to do (and it is strongly implied that he will eventually kill her), she manages to evade him by losing herself in a crowd of actors leaving a theater. The actors invite Jacqueline to join them for a drink, but she declines and makes her way home. She knows that all companionship is temporary and that there is only one way to truly escape the Palladists for good. There is no place she can walk without still being alone.

The Ghost Ship (1943)

Despite its title, *The Ghost Ship* does not have anything to do with ghosts; rather, it is a psychological horror film (made decades before the term "psychological horror" was in use) about a ship's officer who suspects his captain is insane.

The film has two scenes that could be vague analogies to the night walk, but in both cases, they're made significantly weaker by the addition of a soundtrack. In one scene, the officer, Tom Merriam, is investigating the captain's quarters in search of evidence, when he is interrupted by the captain revealing that he was hiding in the shadows, watching him. The second scene occurs near the end of the film, when the captain, Will Stone, begins to realize that his crew is taking Merriam's accusations of madness seriously.

It should be noted that, while neither of these scenes is very powerful, the entire film deals with the theme of solitude. Following the first scene, Captain Stone confidently states that he will take no action against Tom for his perceived insubordination. Rather, he gives Tom the run of the ship, encouraging him to share his theory with his crewmembers. The captain is confident that none of them will help Tom and that he is, for all practical purposes, completely isolated on the ship. It is telling that the first night walk occurs when not a single crewmember will stand against the captain, and the second occurs when the captain realizes that not a single crewmember is left who will stand with him.

The Curse of the Cat People (1944)

After the success of *Cat People*, it only made sense that RKO would want a sequel. Val Lewton took the order for a sequel, as well as the title *The Curse of the Cat People*, and made something both haunting and completely unexpected.

The film takes place several years after the events in *Cat People*. Oliver and Alice have married, gotten a house in the suburbs, and settled into a very normal, horror-free life. Their six-year-old daughter, Amy, is pleasant, but prone to daydreams. These fantasies eventually coalesce into Amy's imaginary friend, Irena, who looks and sounds like Oliver's dead first wife. It is never made clear whether Irena is a ghost or simply a child's fantasy. Either way, Amy's parents grow increasingly concerned about her "friend," culminating in Oliver punishing Amy for insisting that she can see Irena. Amy responds by running away from home, which is when her night walk begins.

As in *Ghost Ship*, Amy's night walk is made less intense by the presence of a soundtrack. Amy's imagination makes threats out of noises she would otherwise find insignificant. For example, the sound of wheels rattling on a cobblestone path hearkens back to a story she heard about the Headless Horseman, even though she soon sees that it is simply a passing automobile. Amy is not accompanied by her imaginary friend on this journey, but she does eventually find sanctuary in the home of Julia Ferren, an old woman who is also scorned for being too imaginative.

The Curse of the Cat People does not fit any standard definition of "horror" film. However, the theme of isolation is still strong, and even the imagination, usually shown as a source of liberation, is shown to be something that can shut people off from one another.

The Body Snatcher (1945)

After producing two non-horror features (*Mademoiselle Fifi* and *Youth Runs Wild*), Lewton returned to RKO's horror line. *The Body Snatcher* was based on a story by Robert Louis Stevenson and starred the two men most synonymous with the blockbuster Universal horror films of the 1930s: Bela Lugosi and Boris Karloff. While Lugosi does the best he can with the sparse part of Joseph, a medical assistant, Boris Karloff shines as John Gray, the body snatcher.

There is one night walk in this film and it lasts for less than a minute, but it still manages to pack a surprising punch. Gray is told that he must procure another body for medical research, but the cemeteries are being guarded, so he is forced to look elsewhere. Considering his dilemma, Gray sees a street singer pass his window and comes to a horrible decision. The camera remains static as the street singer passes, walking into a dark overpass, her song reassuring us that she is alive and well. Gray's horse-drawn cab then follows the singer into the darkness. Her song continues, even as the cab disappears from sight. And then, suddenly, the song is cut off in mid-word. The camera lingers on the dark silent passageway for several seconds before fading to the next scene.

In this case, the street singer feels no fear, and it is the audience that bears the terrible knowledge of her impending fate. She is a peripheral character through the first half of the film, seen frequently but hardly noticed by anyone, making her a solitary character. Her absence is likewise barely noticed, but nevertheless felt.

Isle of the Dead (1945)

Lewton's next film was set on a Greek island in 1912, with the Balkan War serving as a backdrop. The plot concerns nine people, each visiting the island for his or her own reasons, who learn that one of them has contracted septicemic plague. To prevent the plague from spreading to the mainland and potentially infecting thousands of soldiers, they must remain under quarantine until the sirocco winds arrive and dispel it. The superstitious among them suspect a supernatural explanation for their predicament: that one of them is a vorvolaka (a type of vampire).

Near the end of the film, Thea, whom two of the remaining inhabitants believe to be the vorvolaka, decides to go for a walk to find peace in solitude. Everyone else who is still alive remains in the cabin, so Thea has no reason to fear the dark. The sound of the wind is joined by various birdcalls, some that sound like screams and some that sound like singing. One call in particular sounds like a lullaby sung by Mrs. St. Aubyn, the woman who was under Thea's care until she succumbed to the plague. Of course, part of the superstition of the vorvolaka is that anyone who dies from its attack will return as one.

As the singing continues, Thea is followed by a ghostly figure in white. To allay her suspicions, she runs towards the mausoleum where Mrs. St. Aubyn's body was interred. What she finds is perhaps the simplest iteration of quiet horror: an empty tomb.

The shadows of trees outside the mausoleum blend with Thea's own shadow, and, in the flickering, it is unclear whether or not the shadow of another woman can be seen at the doorway. In the light of day, Thea would never believe in things like volvolakas. But when she's taking a night walk . . .

Bedlam (1946)

The last of Lewton's RKO horror films was *Bedlam*, set in the infamous St. Mary's of Bethlehem Asylum in 1761. The story concerns the efforts of George Sims to maintain control over the inmates through cruel, often sadistic means. Opposing him is Nell Bowen, a reformer who wishes to bring about better living conditions. Through subtle maneuvering, Sims arranges to have Bowen herself committed to his asylum.

The only scene in *Bedlam* that even approaches the night walks of earlier films lasts for only half a minute. Hannay, a Quaker and ally in Bowen's crusade, has snuck his way into the asylum to offer her words of hope. As he searches for her, Hannay finds himself walking down an unlit hallway, which he believes is empty. But as he makes his cautious way, hands reach out from the walls, and he realizes that madmen are caged all around him. Again, this scene is made less tense by the presence of a soundtrack.

As a coda to Lewton's work, *Bedlam*, while a fine film in its own right, does not necessarily best display what made his work so unique. He would die five years later in 1951. Fortunately, his legacy would survive his passing and inspire at least two of the directors with whom he worked.

Night of the Demon (1957)

Jacques Tourneur was the director on Lewton's first three films. In 1957, he directed a film that owed a great deal to Lewton's techniques: *Night of the Demon* (released in an edited form in the United States as *Curse of the Demon*). The film is an adaptation of the classic M. R. James ghost story "Casting the Runes." It uses the same heavy reliance on shadow, atmosphere, and ambiguity that made the Lewton-produced films so memorable and effective.

The storyline concerns a sinister mystic, Julian Karswell, and a paranormal debunker, John Holden, who intends to expose Karswell as a fraud who uses his mystic society as a pretense for various confidence and extortion schemes. Karswell responds to Holden's threats by placing a curse on him.

There are two night walks in this film, both done with a minimal soundtrack. First, Holden approaches Karswell's manor with the intention of breaking in and finding documents that detail his schemes. The swaying of tree branches, the whistling of wind, and the barking of unseen dogs can all be heard. It is almost a relief when he enters the dubious safety of the sorcerer's inner sanctum. After a surprisingly casual conversation with Karswell, Holden says that he plans to leave the same way he entered. During the second night walk, the subtle tone is broken as an ever-growing mist follows Holden, the demon apparently lurking deep within it.

There are so many scenes in *Night of the Demon* where a viewer can almost feel the guiding hand of Lewton helping the brilliant Tourneur in evoking something subtler than *Godzilla* or *The Creature from the Black Lagoon*.

The Haunting (1963)

Robert Wise was the director of both *Curse of the Cat People* and *The Body Snatcher*. In 1963, he directed an adaptation of Shirley Jackson's *The Haunting of Hill House*. *The Haunting* is rightly considered one of the greatest horror films of all time and owes a great deal to the influence of Lewton. One area where this is visible is in the presence of the night walk, which plays a central role, and which is presented in multiple iterations.

Quite simply, every time any one of the four main characters walks through Hill House alone, it is a variation of the night walk. The hallways are appropriately shaded, night or day. Mirrors and statues seem to pop up unexpectedly (like the bus scene in *Cat People* repeated over and over). Eleanor Lance in particular seems to be targeted by the house, and it is implied that she is always being watched, even when she is alone. *Especially* when she is alone.

Perhaps the most masterful nod that Robert Wise makes to his former producer is a classic scene in which Eleanor and her fellow investigator, Theodora, are awakened in the night by the sound of footsteps. As they both sit terrified in bed, the sound of footsteps grows ever louder as they thunder down the hallway. These footsteps are followed by a pounding at the bedroom door and then the laughter (or screams) of children receding down the hallway.

The scene is, quite simply, a night walk taken in the opposite direction. The point-of-view characters are relatively motionless, while the darkness walks towards, then past them. When the doorknob slowly begins to turn, they know they cannot stop whatever is on the other side.

Furthermore, Eleanor's character is constantly being isolated from the others, both physically and emotionally. Before she even arrives at Hill House, she is portrayed as being both friendless and at odds with her own family. She is in many ways a woman who has been making night walks all her life, and in fact the invitation to Hill House is a means of escape from that dark life. Her repeated attempts to make social connections with other people (at least living people) are doomed to failure, and when the darkness of Hill House finally consumes her, it is unclear whether or not she welcomes it.

Horror movies are often a communal experience. How many of us gather with friends to enjoy the latest horror film?

But when our friends cannot make it, do we go alone? Do we sit in a room full of strangers and watch the make-believe lives of people who sometimes seem a little too similar to us? Or do we wait until it is available on video, to be watched in the true solitude of our homes? In the dark. We always watch these movies in the dark.

Val Lewton wanted to show audiences those horrible minutes in their lives that they pretend not to remember. After a late shift, when our car is the only one left in the parking lot. When the receptionist tells us the doctor is ready with our results and we just have to cross a hallway to his office. When we wake in the middle of the night and must use the bathroom. When we find ourselves going on a night walk.

"And we who walk here walk alone."
—Eleanor Lance, *The Haunting* (1963)

Bibliography

Bedlam. Directed by Mark Robson. RKO, 1946. Warner Brothers, 2005. DVD.

The Body Snatcher. Directed by Robert Wise. RKO, 1945. Warner Brothers, 2005. DVD.

Cat People. Directed by Jacques Tourneur. RKO, 1942. Warner Brothers, 2005. DVD.

Curse of the Cat People. Directed by Robert Wise. RKO, 1944. Warner Brothers, 2005. DVD.

Ghost Ship. Directed by Mark Robson. RKO, 1943. Warner Brothers, 2005. DVD.

The Haunting. Directed by Robert Wise. Metro-Goldwyn-Mayer, 1963. Warner Home Video, 2010. DVD.

Isle of the Dead. Directed by Mark Robson. RKO, 1945. Warner Brothers, 2005. DVD.

I Walked with a Zombie. Directed by Jacques Tourneur. RKO, 1943. Warner Brothers, 2005. DVD.

The Leopard Man. Directed by Jacques Tourneur. RKO, 1943. Warner Brothers, 2005. DVD.

Martin Scorsese Presents Val Lewton: The Man in the Shadows. Directed by Kent Jones. Warner Home Video, 2005. DVD.

Night of the Demon/Curse of the Demon. Directed by Jacques Tourneur. Columbia, 1957. Sony Pictures Home Entertainment, 2002. DVD.

The Seventh Victim. Directed by Mark Robson. RKO, 1943. Warner Brothers, 2005. DVD.

Shadows in the Dark: The Val Lewton Legacy. Directed by Constantine Nasr. New Wave Entertainment, 2005. DVD.

Vieira, Mark A. "Darkness, Darkness: The Films of Val Lewton: Looking Back at a B-Movie Master." *Bright Lights Film Journal* 50 (November, 2005). http://brightlightsfilm.com/darkness-darkness-films-val-lewton-looking-back-b-movie-master.

Title: Stoned
Artist: Dejan Ognjanović

Infinite Light, Infinite Darkness

By Martin Rose

T̲HE VALLEY curled in on itself, and Võ thought it trapped the people who stumbled into it so they could not leave, for Võ had been trying to leave since his wife and son passed away. Võ granted this condition no mystery, as he must be dead himself to warrant it, and if he was dead and trapped in this valley, so must be the American.

Harvests of rice defined the valley and designed time in the valley, and down in the valley was where Võ found him. Down in the valley, in flooded paddies, Võ thought him dead, yet another dead American soldier face down in the water with snakes burrowing beside him until Võ pulled him up and turned him over and blood erupted from his lips.

The American went for his weapon.

Võ clocked him once in the solar plexus and then the face.

The American collapsed with a breathy squeal from the shadow of his helmet. Blood dribbled from his nose and, with the American's eyes closed, reminded Võ of his long-ago son. The slightness of his youth. And then the old man bit back his agony and heaved the soldier up again and dragged him back to the village. Võ deposited him on a chair inside the hut.

When Võ asked the American if he shouldn't return to his other soldiers, a funny thing happened:

The soldier burst into tears and begged to stay with him.

For the first days, Võ fed and sheltered the soldier. Where Võ slept, he retained a picture of his wife and son folded beside his bed, and the soldier picked it up once and unfolded it in his lap and then returned it and said nothing. All the while, Võ chewed a betel nut until his saliva ran red and thick as blood and kept his eye trained upon him. The empty M-16 sat propped against the wall.

The second day, the soldier woke before him and left the hut. Green shoots trailed above the water line feeding in from the Red River delta outside. Võ joined him to greet the sunrise and noted a deep starvation had taken hold of the soldier, and Võ counted the ribs along his back. A bandanna around the soldier's head kept the hair out of his eyes, soaked up the sweat of the unrelenting humidity while Võ embodied it wholly and wondered how their American skin did not disintegrate in the soupy air.

The soldier scratched at his forehead when Võ looked in the other direction, as though in secret, and this did not escape Võ's notice. He said nothing of it. The soldier refused to speak, and Võ did not rush him.

"If you intend to stay here," he told him at the end of that first week, "I could use your help with the harvest."

The next day, the American took off his dog tags and did not put them back on.

When Võ picked them up to read the name off them, he discovered the soldier's name had been scratched out.

In the middle of the night, the soldier woke him with a cacophony of screams.

Võ rolled out of bed and clapped a hand over the soldier's mouth. The soldier finally drove the blackness out of his own head and awakened to the present. The American's face had grown thick with a beard even though he looked the same age Võ's son would be, had he survived.

"What were you screaming about?" Võ asked.

The soldier scratched at the bandanna over his forehead, at the same space he had been digging and itching at all this while, furtive and restless. He stopped only to return, compulsively, to rub at the same spot with haunted regularity, the space between the eyes. Sat up on the floor and Võ took the chair. Võ's dead son would have sat before him like this. His wife cooking by the fire.

All gone now. Only this soldier remained with his obsessive itching at the space between his eyes, until the soldier spasmed.

His hands and fingers snapped to each other and made a shape, a gesture ringing the bell of memory, the mudra. Võ's son, his long dead son who liked to hear him tell the story. Võ remembers: *amitabha Buddha*.

Before the dreadful day the valley turned red with the eclipse, and Võ came back to his hut to find blood stains on the floor but no wife and no son, there were gentle days of telling his son stories, old folktales, things long forgotten. His son's hands would curl and move, erratic and frenzied when he did not think Võ was looking—at first it was a child's interest in imitating the manner of the statues of the amitabha Buddha, whose story Võ would tell at bedtime. Võ demonstrated the mudra—right hand out, with thumb and forefinger in a circle, the left arm gesturing down with the thumb and forefinger, also touching.

From that moment, his son took the story to heart, wanted to save the unenlightened from themselves, and so felt by gesturing to the insects and the animals that he might be elevating them and preparing his own journey to the future afterlife—but over time, his gestures seemed to mutate, to stray from their original form until it was like no mudra at all, but a new shape.

"Not like that, son," Võ pointed out and corrected him, but his son's face turned red, twisted as he yanked his arm away from him, and Võ could only stare, confused, lost in a sense of vicarious shame for his son's embarrassment.

"Not like that," his son hissed.

"That's not the manner of amitabha."

"The monk showed me a new way."

"Which monk? I've not seen a monk here in ages. There are no temples."

His son shook his head. He scratched at his forehead until a red rash formed in the space above his eyes where his fingers lingered, stroking, scratching, etching at the skin.

"The temple over there," and he pointed. Võ shielded his eyes from the sun but saw nothing in the landscape.

"Who is this monk? What is his name?"

"We don't talk. We sit in the temple, and he shows me things."

Like mudras which are not mudras, show gestures that belong to no compassionate god, thought Võ, but did not say.

Võ went later to the place his son indicated but found nothing; nothing but seething and tangled vines and rotting jungle ground, sinking beneath his feet and ripe with decay. He found his son's footprints but nothing else. Rumors populated every rural town in this country of sites where the local peoples worshipped long before the Buddhists came and took the old temples for their own. By that time, people had forgotten the names of what they worshipped and let those forgotten god stones fall into ruin, left in a place between love and fear, many mistaking one for the other. If there had ever been a temple, it was gone now, and by the time Võ meant to question his son, his son was gone, too.

And now the soldier was here, his hands spasming like Võ's son's in imitation of the mudra, and Võ blurted out:

"Do you mock me?"

The soldier blinked. Perhaps it was an accident of posture, and the soldier sat up and the stance he assumed, echoing that of the long-ago Buddha, fell apart and it was nothing, nothing at all.

The American soldier swallowed and then commenced to speak, in halting stops and starts, drawing Võ from the past to forget the blood stains on his floor, for a little while.

I keep trying to leave this valley. But it doesn't seem to end. It runs in a circle, even upwards and down; dig me? I'm saying I can't get out. I've been trying to get out. I'm scared, old man. Have you been to the temple? Christ, it itches. I'm afraid I'm tearing myself to pieces, bleeding under this rag. I'm afraid to take it off. Been running the circle of this valley, but it's that temple, that goddamned temple. It looks like a Buddhist temple, I think it was a Buddhist temple, but it ain't. It ain't.

Did you know that, old man? We came over here to hold the line against the fighters coming up. They send me out there with an M-16 that jams twenty times to each bullet. They send us out there with wrong coordinates and guess work. They send us out there to die. In hundred plus heat and humidity in full flak jackets that won't do anything to protect us and snipers taking pot shots at us from the trees.

A fire fight at midnight and lost in the jungle. Tracers lighting the sky, and sometimes we get air support and sometimes we don't. I found the temple during a skirmish. Stones all wrapped up in vines and snarled in the trees. Found it by accident. I thought it was a thick shadow I could run through and come out the other side. There was no other side. Endless stone, endless valley. I hit stone, hit it so hard I fell back onto the ground. I stayed there, dazed and staring at a sky filled with tracers zipping past the milky way. Obliterated moon. Bullets shredding foliage and machine gun fire all around me.

I didn't have the strength to go back to the battle. I got up against my will and fell against the stone, watered it with my tears, when I found a door.

I entered the temple, tears forgotten.

A curtain of leaves and vines closed behind me like I had passed through a membrane. My ears rang with explosions and they popped when I entered. Inside, the temple opened into a great hall. Stones sweated with humidity under a huge blackness. A monk occupied the altar. Legs crossed in his orange robes. He was meditating in the middle of a fire fight roaring outside and shaking the ground. Eyes closed. Head shaved and still against the backdrop of stone.

The atmosphere hushed. My presence unwanted. I thought to steal a second or a minute of time and then be gone forever to leave this old man to his philosophy and chasing the mysteries of life and death. Instead, I drifted in and sat down across from him. My mission to return to the fire fight with the medic forgotten. Time betrayed me. I set my M-16 down on the ground. My murder weapon was a sacrificial offering.

I could stay here, I realized. I told myself I would return, a moment's rest, and then back to the fire fight.

Seconds became minutes, minutes became hours.

By the time I understood the fight was over, I couldn't remember how I came to the temple in the first place.

When the fire fight ended, I went back to the infantry and told them I got tangled up in a side conflict. They swallowed the lie and never guessed anything different.

When the fighting arrived again, I ran for the temple. I sneaked inside and kneeled before the monk, and the monk was always there. Sometimes he smelled like oranges. He never spoke to me or acknowledged me. I began to feel like he and I shared some secret, this crack in the world where the temple was forgotten. Surely it was thousands of years old. It would see a thousand years more. It saw the French come and go. It saw the Viet Cong. It saw the Americans. And we were just a long string of endless people with no concrete effect and no benefit to the country, to the land, to the people.

I looked for the temple on our maps and civilian maps. But there are places in the world where the geography is uncharted and camouflaged. Maybe an old man like you may know of this temple. Or your ancestors before you who kept it secret and guarded. That's the nature of places with power. They exist in a knot of ley lines that conspire to vanish their location, saturate them in shadows, bury them in the hidden crevices of the earth.

But every time the growl of the guns began, I found my way to it. And I started to leave my gun outside and take my helmet off. I came as a supplicant, as a lover. I gave up my armor and my martial aspect. Took off my boots to cool my rotting and crushed bare feet against the stone. I abandoned the flaming world behind me for a one-room universe without blood and pain. Relieved me of my ringing ears and my shaking, my flinching, my endless suffering. Relieved me of memories of others fallen and others I couldn't save.

I took my place beside the monk.

Peace stole into my heart and put out the fires.

And I did this, over and over again.

I made up stories of my disappearances, fabricated excuses. In all that noise and confusion, nobody questioned why I came and went at such odd moments. People I fed these lies to died by the next fire fight, died before they could report my curious absence. I went unnoticed and unloved. An odd effect took hold—other soldiers swore they saw me in battle. That I appeared and disappeared at key moments in-country. Some thought I died, and then they reported me alive again in the next breath.

I knew it was just a matter of time before my lie was discovered, my secret hiding place found out.

The day I killed the spider, the monk moved for the first time.

The spider tumbled from the stone and skittering over hanging vines. My reaction was automatic. It was ingrained by years of habit. It said volumes about my carelessness, about my wretched, destroying heart. My fist came down, impacted with a sound like gunfire, and the spider's guts and all his eyes stared up from the tangle of his limbs. His fine hairs and his waving fangs. Maybe it was a she. Maybe she carried eggs in her belly. Maybe she was heavy with a thousand more like her, genocide by the handful. But the air, so soupy and dense in this temple, was like a tomb.

I wiped the gore and pulp on my pant leg.

When I looked, the monk's eyes were open. He stared at me. Eyes turned brilliant, glowing mandalas of brown and yellow above his orange robe.

He raised one finger to his lips. I thought at last he might speak. He didn't. He shook his head in disapproval and then closed his eyes and seemed to fold in on himself and back into the realms of his interior space. An origami design of carbon and skin.

The spider's fine hairs tickled my fingers. Its burning blood was a stain I couldn't get rid of. If I thought it was hot before in the humid air, I turned even hotter in the rush of shame as I went all scarlet in the darkness of the temple. I destroyed the sanctity of this place with one thoughtless, careless act. I spent so many of my days and nights struggling not to think about anything at all while I was pushed and pulled between one fire fight and the other. I suddenly had a vivid recollection. My long-ago childhood. My youth I had forgotten.

I remembered my father reading *The Odyssey* to me in his cabin in the woods, in front of a roaring fire. I remember the island of the cows and how they slaughtered by accident what they should have held sacred. And they paid for it.

I watched the monk for a while longer; and after a while, I thought, *Let it go.* Just a feeling. It was a mere spider. This sense of trespass, of wrongness, will pass.

Before long, the monk and I would meet again in this place, with bullets ringing against the stone outside and the jungle burning with napalm.

The next day, a red welt bloomed on the flesh of my hand where I hit the spider. Another appeared, growing red and angry in the space between my eyes.

I scratched at it and wondered if I had transferred the venom to my face by accident or if it had bitten me in secret. The itch and the fire under the skin became incessant, insatiable. I scratched in my sleep and scratched on patrol and on point. People laughed about it, but a sharp shooting pain seethed under the skin and burrowed deep as a snake bite and gave me no rest.

We were called out to the valley to intercept a crew of guerillas. While the other men forged ahead, I lagged behind and judged their lapse in vigilance so I could sidestep into the jungle. I parted the leaves and ran away into my beloved temple with the spot in my skin growing angry and big as a dime.

Inside the temple at last, the burn and sting of the itch dimmed. The relief made me cry. I took off my boots at the door in a show of respect. My bloody and broken feet gone to fungus with jungle rot. I laid them on the cool stones. The entrance was like a mouth and the floor was like a tongue to lap at my wounds.

In its center, the monk.

I had been coming here so often now, the sound of the fire fight in the valley muted to my senses, an inconvenient background noise. I stared at his face—wide as a moon. His eyes, ended up up-tilted seams. The nose, flattened and pushed into his face. For all the slurs of the other soldiers who sneered out racial epithets, this monk's face had become like a brother's. I couldn't remember the last time I looked into a mirror. My own face faded into memory and his face was my face and each of us reflecting endlessly into the other. Of course, I had always been here. There had never been anything before this temple. There had never been a life overseas in some smoggy industrialized first-world wasteland called America, populated with monstrous apes who'd escaped the trees and been set loose, raping and murdering and throwing shit and calling it civilization.

I had always been here. There had never been a time before and never a time after and all of life and light one unending moment.

I lost myself. Do you know that? I lost myself. And I loved it. I didn't regret kneeling on that stone with that monk and taking my place beside him.

I forgot to return when the fire fight was ended.

In this way, I made my error.

The itching returned to my forehead with a ferocity no inner peace could soothe. It forced me to hang the bandanna around my scalp to prevent me from debriding the skin. I'd carved a place with my fingernails until jagged lines ran down the front of my forehead with blood dripping into my face. Still no relief.

While I sat with the monk, I heard the door of the temple open.

A man called my name.

I didn't move. His heavy combat boots, caked with mud, left outlines on the blessed stone in the shape of an insult. I wanted him to go. I recognized his voice and had known him. I could smell the stick of gum he kept in his pocket; the tobacco in his cigarettes. I snarled when I realized he'd brought instruments of violence in this, my holy place.

"Oh shit, thank god you're here! Thought the VC got you, and man, Pinchot is such a fucker, he'd leave you out there. Hey man, you all right?"

I rose from the stones and turned to face Winn, Pfc Kenny Winn. I culled memories from another age of this soldier who had once been my brother in arms. If I closed my eyes I could call up each of those memories like a stack of cards I turned lazily in hand—Winn telling annoying knock-knock jokes on the ride up to base camp. Winn showing us a letter from his sister. When he was ten, he shot a raccoon because it contracted rabies and cried. The others made unmerciful fun of him for it because *what do you think you're here to do, you dumb fuck, if you can't even shoot a raccoon.*

A strange thing happened then, with my eyes closed.

I realized I could see Winn without opening my eyes.

And I could pull more than memories from that stack of cards. I pulled the memories of things yet to happen and things yet to be.

Winn, with blood flowing out of his mouth, the crushed spider, legs twitching. A poor rice farmer in the valley with a picture of a dead wife, a dead son. The monk, staring at me. The *future*.

I was not ready to know this. I put the cards back, hasty and desperate. Images reshuffled. I opened my eyes to the present.

The shadow of the monk carved a serpentine path between us without ever moving at all. He had no time for us and was lost to a secret enlightenment of his own and he was not sharing.

"You gotta come back," Winn said. "Come back with me."

"No."

"What? They're gonna wanna know what happened to you. You can't do that. Whattaya wanna stay out here in some rice paddy for? Come on, stop joking."

"I'm not coming back with you, Winn. I'm home now."

"Is this it? This . ." and Winn began to put it together, faster through his quickening senses as he stared up at the cavernous ceiling and dangling vines. "This is where you've been while we've been fucking out there in the boonies *dying*? This is where you've been hiding?"

I nodded. Winn lunged for me.

The man who cried once when he killed a raccoon came for me with murder in his eyes. I crouched with my hands over my head while he pummeled me and knocked me to the floor. His fists bearing fury with little substance. I could do no more but prostrate myself on the ground. Consider this miserable life of blood and stone.

He unslung his M-16 and brought it up and around.

Winn was going to kill me.

A calm descended.

The monk watched without moving. In the feeble torchlight, his figure buzzed and hummed with unreal intensity—the way the moon moves when you're not looking.

Winn pressed the trigger.

Between the Vietnam heat and the mud and the monsoons, the weapon jammed.

Winn screamed and threw it from him. The rifle skittered across the stones and bounced off a wall and I vaulted from the ground. I felt weightless enough to walk across clouds. To bounce through the stratosphere and into the cosmos. I brought up the thin edge of a knife blade and sank it into Kenny's neck.

He spurted on the floor and blood bubbled up through his lips like an uncorked champagne bottle. I watched him while he stood there grabbing at his throat to close it at the seams and cursed at me. He tried to press out words that meant nothing in the long view but meant a great deal to him. Things about honor and country and the sad summation of his brief and useless life.

He collapsed to the floor at my feet. My jungle rot toes, sticky with his blood.

I looked at the monk. But he was gone from there and I had to leave. Others would be coming to find me.

Võ leaned back and pushed a betel nut in the soldier's direction. The soldier hesitated and then accepted it. Soon, he would salivate a deep and dark red like blood; his teeth blackened the way Võ's had blackened.

"I know this temple," Võ said. "It has been abandoned for many years. You say there was a monk there?"

The soldier looked up. The tips of his fingers trembled on the table.

"Just one. Always the same one."

"No monk would go there, friend. There's nothing there."

"I tell you, there was a monk."

Võ did not argue. He also did not tell him that some Buddhas are worshipped by sacrifice, villagers would pour the blood of gutted animals over ancient stones. Perhaps these were gods posing as imitations for the locals, happily glutted on their share of tribute. A silence filled out with a sigh from the American. The persistent itch of his fingers scratching at the bandanna in the center of his forehead.

When Võ awoke the next morning, the American soldier was gone.

Võ thought he should be relieved; this problem was no longer in his care. But the ruined dog tags still hung beside the bed. They rested with the picture of Võ's son who never came back.

Võ pulled on his shirt. He paused on the threshold of his hut and stared at the blood stains, ossified into the wood. Then, he withdrew a pistol from a blanket, a weapon that once belonged to a French soldier he killed long ago, and then he trudged through the paddy, in the direction of the temple.

Võ listened to the jungle surrounding the rice field. Listened for the sound of American air support or assault rifle reports. But all remained quiet except for the sound of other war-ravaged families of the young and the old tending their paddies. He missed his wife and the way she softened the world by existing in it. The rains were on the way.

He took the path through the rice fields and down into the valley. The fighting ran fierce here, once, but now there was only silence as though this place had become a tomb, the valley an empty coffin. The American forces had moved on. Chasing trails and figments of their colonization. The growing pains of an imperial empire.

Võ knew the way. He traipsed through and entered the jungle's heart, eclipsed into the trees and sent snakes and birds sprawling out of his way and then he waited in the shadow of the temple.

A scream echoed from within.

Võ moved faster. He thought of his son. His wife's absence left a wound in his heart that he salved some nights with memories, but his son's ghost wouldn't—*couldn't*—seem to leave. The pain stayed there in his lungs, so he breathed the name of his family waiting for it to pass, and it did not, and it led him here, before the door of the temple with the gun in his sweating hand and his heart in his mouth, eating his pain back down his throat.

He held the gun steady in one hand and then pressed the door open with the other.

Võ made no noise in his approach. From the inner chamber blew a cold polar wind. A great cavern opened to swallow him and Võ held his breath. They used to dare each other to come here as kids, and he remembered why. Upward the stone columns climbed, but only so far, until the stone vanished, and the very seams of midnight replaced it. Blinding daylight predominated outside, but inside the temple time spun an endless clock face like a compass, and spun back again, to point always to midnight.

In his disorientation, Võ's sense of direction and time juddered. He cleared his vision and gripped the gun but felt, as he crossed the threshold, the offense of this weapon of war. He forced himself to focus while above him the ceiling expanded and exploded into never-ending blackness where vines snaked and intertwined like reptiles above.

Inside the temple, Võ saw his son kneel before the altar.

Beyond him, the great stone Buddha rising from the ground.

Võ blinked, and his son shimmered and disappeared, only an illusion after all, and in his place, the American soldier, whose ribs had filled out these many weeks under Võ's care as he fed at his table, ate of his rice, replaced him.

At either side of him, the soldier was held and restrained by his American compatriots, and Võ hesitated on the threshold in his invisible darkness, holding the space for the right time and the right moment.

The American soldier's face cleaved the darkness with blood and skin, cut and bruised where they had beat him. A thread of hatred unraveled in Võ. He took aim and placed the muzzle over the first soldier's face and he knew he should kill the man, kill him for the blood running from the wound in the soldier's scalp. For the bruises. For the black eyes. For how they held him down and ground him into the stone by his knees.

One soldier leaned down over him and cast a slant of color over the American's upturned face, his lips pulled down into a bloody tragedy mask. The head soldier tasked to bring him back as a traitor with his M-16 hanging over his shoulder leaned over him, ran a thumb over the American's split lip, and the American shook his head *no please don't,* and then the soldier tugged at the bandanna over the boy's forehead.

Võ hesitated. He watched, mesmerized.

"No, don't!"

The American writhed and rocked in the grip of the others as the soldier stepped between Võ's view and yanked the bandanna down. Võ's line of sight was blocked and he could not see but hear the soldier shrieking beneath the gaze of the Buddha beyond him, who held one hand in perfect poise, offering a compassion none of them were capable of taking.

The first one fell face first into the stone. His teeth broke off and skittered across the floor. They still moved like marbles by the time Võ shot the second, and the third. Võ did not stop to think about what he did, for he would surely miss; he kept before him the name and memory of his loved ones. He kept before him the image of his only son, so when the last soldier fell, all that remained was the American soldier panting and crying and huddled on the floor.

Võ surveyed the damage. His bare feet loud on the stones. The Buddha watched without comment or judgment. There was no monk to be found here.

"Up," he commanded.

But the soldier held his head in his hands and would not move.

"Up!" and Võ grabbed him by the arm and yanked him to his feet. The soldier stumbled and Võ smacked his hands away so he stared, with his face naked before him, his eyes red rimmed and swimming in tears. A monsoon flooding down his face.

Between his eyes, set in his forehead like a gemstone, a vertical slit of flesh.

The place he had been itching and worrying with every swipe of his fingers, revealed. A cicatrix puckered down the center. The boy huffed sobs out of his mouth, and when he looked at Võ, the scar twitched.

Võ stepped back and lifted the gun on the American.

The soldier cried harder.

The scar opened. Labial. Moist.

An eye stared out from the scar that was not a scar but an eyelid.

All three of the soldier's eyes studied Võ and as Võ lifted the firearm, to his horror, the third eye wept. Tears hesitated like jewels in his lashes and Võ made out every tiny hair of the third eye.

"Go," Võ commanded.

"Please, please, don't send me away –"

"Go from here."

"I can't go back like this! I have no home! Let me stay with you."

Võ leveled the gunsight over the third eye and it flinched in unison with the other two.

"*Go.*"

The soldier took in a shuddering breath and scuttled away in the darkness and out the door.

Võ released the gun. It fell to the floor.

He stared at the Buddha and went to his knees. Bowed his head.

When he opened his eyes, the stone Buddha was gone. A monk occupied his place.

Võ wondered if he survived at all, if his son and his wife were not waiting for him back at the hut. If this was one bardo, he was lost in among the many; if maybe the American was his son in new form, and this was how he lost him, over and over again. One illusion cascading upon the others.

A spider crawled across his naked feet. Võ did nothing to disturb it but let it pass with its hairy legs some might find despicable and ugly, as some Americans might find Võ with his teeth black from the betel nut despicable and ugly; as someone found his son and wife despicable and ugly and crushed them, as the American soldier who could never replace his son crushed the spider.

It moved away into the darkness unmolested.

The monk nodded with an incline of his head. Võ was filled with relief. After so long trapped in this endless valley, he had arrived here at last.

There was no need to meander in this endless gyre of pain anymore, no more wandering through the bardo of death and war and the ghosts of the ones he loved.

He took a breath. Bowed before the monk, this old god masquerading as a new one, long forgotten until his son stumbled upon him. Until a soldier found him. And now, Võ, who shivered in anticipation of feeling the itch burning at the center of his forehead, the burning crawl at his skin from the underside of his feet, and the monk, who gestured with one hand, offered him gentle enlightenment and relief. On the other, the unknown.

Võ readied himself to be reborn, where light could not follow, swallowing it up through the burning eye forming at the center of his head, like the soldier who could not suffer the fear and instead fled, stumbling and crying and screaming through the endless valley, begging to be released.

Infinite darkness awaited.

Nervous Wares & Abnormal Stares

by Devin Goff

CRIME SCENE EVIDENCE # 553999
COLLECTED 05/1/2014
DEAR DIARY ENTRIES OF DECEASED
TRANSCRIBED BY M. ADLEMAN 12/02/2014

6/2/07
Grand Opening Today!! Lots of customers and great neighbors! I know Ceramics and Sundries will be a success. I have to admit moving to Old Alton was nerve-wracking, but today's crowd showed me I was worried for nothing! Saturday isn't a typical day to open but the exception has to be made in a small town. No competition helps too! If I can keep this up, I'll be out of debt in no time.

    Eventually I'll rent out this apartment above the store and have another stream of income and get a real house. I might buy one in town. Real estate is tough here. No one's selling! A good sign!! Everyone was so sweet today, I should have asked about all those orange flags I kept seeing and that weird symbol. But since I just arrived I'm sure I'll get the scoop soon.

6/4/07

During lunch I went across the street to Nancy Fancy Nails. The lavender sparkles is my color. Nancy did a good job. I asked about those orange flags, but she and the other ladies went all quiet like I'd asked if they were menstruating or something. Who knows maybe they were? It might be the local school color. When I told them how much I loved their little town I didn't get much of a response. Just Monday blahs I guess.

6/8/07

Business is still consistent. Been a great week. After work I stopped by Pay Less Video to rent Grease. Love that movie!! I'll be singing those songs all day tomorrow in the shop I just know it! I'm surprised there weren't many customers on a Friday night. Maybe everyone heads to the bigger cities for fun?

6/9/07

Slow today compared to last week's opening. Only two customers. I went ahead and closed early and rushed over to Mable Peabody's Beauty Parlor. I had to do something with my hair. Got an interesting little tidbit. Sheriff Thompson disappeared yesterday. Never met him, but they say he ran away with some local young thing but wouldn't say who. Got the feeling Mable and her friends weren't being totally honest.

Maybe that's just because I'm new and don't really know them.

I asked if not having a sheriff was going to be a problem. I mean the crime rate here should be small, it is a small town. They laughed off my question but never answered it. Seems like everyone in town has a secret they're not willing to give up. They see me as an outsider. Things will change.

6/11/07

A new sheriff already? What if Sheriff Thompson comes back? The new one is younger. Heard his name was Windsor. Hopefully he won't disappear either. Got a large order from Mrs. Camdam today. Mainly fall decorations like pumpkins of different sizes and trees dropping leaves, even a large turkey. This will keep the kiln fired up for several weeks. Good thing too. Started to get worried that business would fall off. Maybe after I'm done with this order I can convince her to place an order for some Christmas decorations.

8/6/07

Mrs. Camdam picked up her order today. Besides her only a few small orders here and there. I was hoping she'd place a new order for Christmas, maybe not as big an order but something. She told me she was moving away. She's been my best customer so far. I had to pry. She said it was because of the tumerfron (?) order, whatever that meant. Mrs. Camdam didn't order anything called tumerfron. Was thinking it was a type of pumpkin, but there is no such word in the dictionary. She was adamant about leaving. It's a shame. I need to drum up a fall sale.

8/13/07

The only grocery store in town is closing! I can't believe it! Piggly Wiggly wasn't much of a store but it will be missed. Will have to drive further to pick up groceries now. I hope this isn't a sign of things to come. If a big store can't make it, how is my little shop going to prosper? This news on the heels of no customer orders would normally worry me, but got to take the bad with the good equally as mama always said.

Nancy told me Lance Henderson, the owner of the Piggly

Wiggly, had to close because he was moving away. Said his cattle were attacked and couldn't sell the beef. I would think he'd have a backup plan. Since I'm not a rancher I'm not even sure how all that works anyway. Closing the doors on the September 5. Only Monday but I think I need to rent Grease again.

8/14/07
Went ahead and bought Grease today. Why? Pay Less Video is closing on September 5 too! They're selling off all their videos. Treated myself to a strawberry malt at Candie's Malt and Candy Shoppe. I still feel down and I'm sure I've gained ten pounds because of it. Not every place is closing. Maybe once the weather changes everything will get better.

10/8/07
Starting to have steady customers. Glad it's finally fall. This summer was rough. My nephew Christopher's birthday is a couple of weeks away. I'll sneak over to DSHT Comics across the street and Glen's Toyland next door. I'm sure I'll find something he'd love. I may go by Nancy's too to treat myself. Never really noticed it before but there sure are several places for children here that are enjoyable. A comics store, a toy store, and of course Candie's. Is that typical for small towns? Mama told me she grew up in a small town. I should ask her.

Need to try that restaurant El Sancho's. The whole time I've been here I've never gone. Never cared for Mexican food or spicy food in general for that matter. They'll probably have something without all the spices. I'll go Saturday after I close up the store.

10/13/07
If that isn't all crazy! Went to El Sancho's after work, like I'd planned and turns out they closed! Went to Candie's instead and got a malt and a burger. Like I needed it. Gained a few more pounds.

Goodbye school girl figure! I'll miss you! I'll get back in shape. AFTER the holidays!

Anyways wrapped up Christopher's presents this evening. The DSHT Comics owner Victor recommended several titles I didn't recognize. Looked like scary stuff to me but he said the kids love it. Glen was helpful too. Both of them said they were having sales coming up for Christmas, so I'm sure if Christopher loves what he gets, he'll be a happy camper for Christmas too.

10/31/07

Happy Halloween! I'm glad I stopped by Candie's for extra candy. Got swamped with trick-or-treaters. What's weird is most of them were dressed the same. Long orange robes with hoods. Must be an Old Alton tradition. It kind of freaked me out a little. Nobody played any tricks so it's harmless fun.

11/3/07

Don't know what's going on, but DSHT Comics closed their doors today. Where is everyone going? The town isn't that bad, is it? With all the children I saw on Halloween, there must be lots of disappointment going around. At least Glen's Toyland is still open! I think I'll do another sale. Maybe that will cheer everyone up.

11/21/07

Heading to my sister's place for Thanksgiving tomorrow. In a way, I'm relieved to get out of town. Sounds awful to say but something strange is happening but can't put my finger on it. Think it's just my weight gain that has me down. Eating turkey and desserts won't help I know. After the holidays, I promise.

12/2/07

One of the only places in town open on Sundays closed today. And so near Christmas too. I asked Glen why he's closing but never got a clear answer. Been here six months, and I'm still treated like a stranger. What's up with that?

12/25/07
Merry Christmas! I'm closing for the rest of the year. Just a week left anyway. Nancy invited me over to her family's house. I'll head there before going to my sister's. Mable invited me to her place too. At least I have a couple of friends now! It only took six months! Mama always said I was impatient!

5/8/08
Was going to write in my diary everyday but I let that slip like my weight. Candie's closed her doors today. Didn't want to finish up the week. Considering all the places that closed last year I'm not surprised. Haven't seen too many children around lately. Maybe it's because it's the end of the school year?

6/2/08
Officially open a whole year. Even with other businesses closed Ceramics and Sundries is still in the black. Barely but maybe with all the available store fronts new businesses will move in and the town grow. I remain hopeful!

6/7/08
Can't believe it! Nancy closed her doors today! She didn't say anything to me. Not even goodbye! Some friend. I've still got Mable. Lost five pounds since Monday. That's something.

8/5/08
Yesterday was decent. Bad news today. Mable closed. Couldn't even finish out the week. Who's going to do my hair now? That garage and tow place is still open. Are they next? Where have all the children gone? No birds either. Am I next?

9/19/08

The orange folk picked up their statue today, just in time too. I was about to close for the day. Been a long week. Oh yeah, I never described this group in any entry before. They dressed like those trick-or-treaters last year. Orange robes, hoods, very cult-ish looking, all had the same tattoo. It was of that strange symbol I keep seeing around town. There were six of them but four never said a word to me.

They all had this blank expression. Sunken eyes. Like none of them had slept in days. Made me nervous around my ceramics. Didn't want them falling over and breaking anything. Were they on drugs? I hope not. Don't want any trouble.

Weeks ago, they asked for a ceramic statue. It was creepy, but I did it anyway. Needed the money. They paid enough to keep me in the black for the rest of the year as long as I didn't tell anyone about it. Who am I going to tell? All my friends have moved away!

I don't like to see it again but here's a sketch on the following page:

(PAGE TORN OUT)

Disgusting I know but with that payday I'm not going to complain. Whoever came up with that design had a good imagination. To tell the truth making that thing upset my stomach bad. When I drew it just now, it gave me chills. Don't know why. It's just a stupid statue.

Had to make it in a weird way too. They said I could only work on it between the hours of two and four in the morning. I told them that's not my working hours. But they insisted I follow their instructions to the letter or they wouldn't pay.

Who am I to argue? Business has about dried up anyway, so I did it. When they came by today and saw the completed statue they actually smiled. What creeps! Before they left they said they'll come back every year and pay me even more money to make more of those statues. Yeah right. I need a vacation!

6/2/09
Two years open and I think I'll be closing soon. Hardly any customers. If it wasn't for that money I got last year from those weirdoes I'd already be closed. The orange folk never returned like they promised. Don't know if that's a good thing or bad thing. Given how I remember feeling and the odd hours I worked, I'd say it's a good thing. I didn't mention it, but I had scary dreams the whole time that statue was in my store downstairs. Don't remember them and don't want to.

I might stay open for another month while I look for a new place. Maybe a bigger town would be better. Old Alton is a ghost town. No. Ghosts don't even live here now. At least I'm losing weight. I'll keep that up.

7/13/09
They came for their statue today. Yeah, the orange folk returned. It was bigger than the last one I built for them. I was given even more money than last year. I can't believe it. Living off just one group of customers isn't so bad. The boredom is driving me crazy. Or maybe it's that statue?

I dreamt of a cloaked figure like that group. Only this one was ten feet tall. I don't know why I'm dreaming about them. It was too disturbing to remember the details. I'd wake up drenched in sweat and out of breath like I'd been working out. I need to work out. Take my mind off it all.

2/19/10
The people with the abnormal stares got another statue today. Bigger than the last two I made. What are the orange folk doing with these things? Looks like it's used for some sort of ritual. Could

they be Satanists or something? Am I contributing to the downfall of mankind?

Get real girl. It's probably some monument to Comic-Con. Those weirdoes will do anything to freak out normal people. They're just being lame. Happy it's Friday. I'm not going to bother opening tomorrow. I keep thinking I'm going to close permanently but this money influx keeps changing my mind.

6/2/10

Hadn't been opened in months. Ceramics and Sundries is so dusty. I decided to clean up and open the doors for the three-year anniversary. Naturally no one showed up. Not even Sheriff Windsor or that garage and tow owner, Julie Capra, came. See if I ever take my car to that garage!

I think those two were or are an item. Don't know. They keep to themselves. Of course, I keep to myself too. They probably think I'm a crazy lady. I watch Grease over and over. The only thing that makes me happy.

Been thinking about it, where do the orange folk come from? They act local, but I've never seen any of them. Do they really live here or is it an annual thing? Maybe they keep to the woods. Don't think I'm going to stay open. Time to move. Even ghosts get tired of haunting after a while.

3/12/11

The orange folks got their statue again. The biggest one yet. I only stay open for them. Why don't I move? For the promise of their money? Only once a year. Each time it's taken me longer to make it.

It's not just the birds and the children who've gone away. Bugs. Not a one around. Am I so gross looking not even flies want to buzz me?

That thing kept staring at me. I know it was. It must be alive.

After I baked it in the kiln, I covered its face with a tissue for the paint job and I swear it could still see me. Following me around with its eyes. It wants to kill me. I don't think I could build another one. I'd go crazy-crazy. Afraid to leave the apartment. What if it follows me like its eyes?

Oh God, what are they doing with these things? Why do they keep getting bigger and bigger? Are they eventually going to want a life-size one? One ten feet tall like that figure in my dreams? Am I losing my mind?

6/2/11

Year four! I really should move. Came across a bizarre coincidence. Hope it's a coincidence. Maybe I'm just bored. It's the dates. Flipped through this diary the other day and noticed an odd pattern. Maybe I'm just seeing something that isn't there from 2007. Piggly Wiggly and Pay Less Video closed on 9/5. Mrs. Camdam moved on 8/6. Looking back further on 6/8 Sheriff Thompson disappeared. All these dates add up to 14.

I saw it again in 2008. 5/8 Candie's closed, 6/7 Nancy's closed, 8/5 Mable closed! They add up to 13! Is my mind just trying to see order where there is none? When there's nothing else to do, this is what I do. Who wouldn't be curious about it? Just a game to whittle my headspace. No harm in playing games. Wonder if it has anything to do with those strange orange folk? I'll look further.

Nope. The dates when they showed up to get their statue thing splat that theory! Whew! I'm excited about that.

(ILLEGIBLE)

(MATH EQUATIONS?)

It's counting down 37 then 31 then 25 then 19. Next should be 13. 1/7, 2/6, 3/5, 4/4, 5/3, or 6/2. If they show up on any of these six dates, I'll know I'm not crazy! Even if the orange folks never show up again and prove I'm getting a little nutty I won't mind. I hope they don't show. I must be loopy waiting to find out if they'll return.

1/7/12

I'm really scared. I was right. Still shaking and they left hours ago. The countdown is now at 13. What does that mean? What happens when it gets down to one? Wait. Think about it, you silly goose! How can any date equal one? Maybe it's the last I'll see of them. Of course! I'll never see them again. I've thought that before though.

Their statue is now five feet tall. A little shorter than me. Something eerie is going on and thought of it just now. Never brought it up before but the orange folk always gave me instructions on how to build it like the amount of ceramic mix to use, the paints, colors and such. For every single one I've built I've always used the same amount!! How can it get bigger? I'm almost in a trance when I built those things. Why don't I ever write in this diary the day they come to tell me when they'll need it? I write in this on the day they pick it up.

Just touching those things affects me. My nerves have tittered on safety when building and painting other ceramic figurines because I don't want to break them. But those statues of that evil thing are my true nervous wares. Not afraid of breaking them but afraid they will come to life and slash me with those claws. In a way, I hope I break one.

What am I saying? How would the orange folk react if I break one of their little gods? Is that what it is? A god? Should I just pack and leave? I need to stop writing this and put on some Grease. That will cheer me up.

6/1/12

Just a day short of my five-year anniversary. Has it been that long? I've packed up the store and all my stuff. It is moving day. Yep finally leaving this damned town. I might have gained over a hundred pounds since I arrived yet when I was going to pack my bathroom scale I weighed myself and I've lost 150 pounds! I'm smaller now than when I first came here. The ghost town diet. Ha!

My nerves can't take it anymore. Goodbye Old Alton. Mama will be glad to see me again. Frankly I'll be happy to see her.

6/4/12

It's a great Monday! I moved in with Mama for just a couple of weeks until I get my own place. She was worried about my weight loss, but she had to admit I look good! I may burn this to forget about that awful period in my life. Not sure what I'll do but I have enough money I saved to open a new store. Don't think I want to go that route again. Will think about the possibilities. Got plenty of time!

12/13/13

Don't know how the orange folk found me. Even mama doesn't know where I live. Built it in the garage. Good thing the ceiling is eight feet in there. They were able to haul it away.

It's 13 again. 1+2+1+3+2+0+1+3=13. Will it just repeat at 13 until it reaches life size? Ten feet. Can't hold out that long can I? That means 5/1/2014 will be 13. 5+1+2+0+1+4=13. What happens then?

Keep dreaming of the tall one. Or I hope it's a dream. I always find the hooded freak at the end of my bed when I wake up. Then I pass out. It's just a dream. Not real. Why do they haunt me? Pick on someone else! If I stop building them would that stop the evil forces from coming through?

Coming through what? I don't know. Just rambling now. The orange folk with their abnormal stares and pale faces will always come back. At least I know when they'll return.

I'm scared. Oh mama I'm so scared.

4/30/14
Finished it. In the backyard this time. They'll find it.

Can't miss it! When it talked to me just a little while ago I finally understood everything. Makes sense. 3/02/2015 is the next one. Freedom. Won't be around to see it though.

I'm going to go away for a little while. Maybe the Orange folk will take this diary when they take the Orange Lord? Don't want mama to see what I've written. I hesitate to destroy this record. Everyone will be deluded enough to think I'm dead.

(ILLEGIBLE)

I won't be dead. I go to the lair. When the sun swallows the moon and the moon swallows the earth and the earth becomes Orange, Orange will rule all. Orange. The mighty and great Orange. Orange. Orange. Orange you glad to see me? Orange.

(ILLEGIBLE)

Orange minus 13 equals life. The Orange Lord showed me eternity. Mama would be proud. My purpose is true. My purpose is Orange. Orange. Orange. Orange. Orange. Orange. Orange. Orange.

(ILLEGIBLE)

Why isn't my blood Orange? Looking for it now. The Orange is hidden but I'll find it. See?

(SMEARED WITH BLOOD STAINS)

I found the ORANGE! So pretty!
(ILLEGIBLE)
My intestines are ORANGE!

ORANGE IS THE WORD!

(ILLEGIBLE)

Much Love to

(ILLEGIBLE)

The Tumerfron Order of the Orange Lord
Orange is my color now!

(SMEARED WITH BLOOD STAINS)

(ILLEGIBLE)

        – END OF TRANSCRIPTION –

Title: Lepidopterium
Artist: Patricia Allison

My Time at the Drake Clinic

By Jordan Krall

"DO YOU think there is a connection between my psychic masochism and the disease?" a student in the back row asked.

"I don't know if there is enough recent research to suggest that, but I suppose it's possible," I replied.

"Anything is possible, right? I mean, I can be sitting here, and the disease can be causing me to ask these questions and therefore causing the masochism to get worse. That can even make the disease get stronger and make it spread even more."

"Let's not jump to conclusions about these things," I said. "You are obviously very self-aware, and that's a step in the right direction."

"I'm not aware at all."

"Oh?"

"No, I don't even know where I am. I don't even know who

you are. All I can remember is opening my eyes and seeing your face in the front of the class, and then I had an urge to ask a question. I'm starting to think that this 'disease' is nothing more than the true incarnation of what people would call 'original sin,' like when the demiurge tempted Adam . . . "

There were murmurs from the other students.

"Okay, quiet down everyone," I said. "Let me try to explain. First, this has nothing to do with the concept of original sin or religion. I think this is a clear example of mild loop panic . . . "

At that point I was interrupted by another student. She was a young woman with multiple scars on her face. "I think he's lying," she said. "I think he already knew the answer to his question before he even asked you. He just likes pretending to be more important than he is. He likes to pretend he's some diseased messiah."

"Let's not jump to conclusions," I said. "We want to give everyone the benefit of the doubt. We all have issues to deal with, but right now I'm teaching you about the background of . . . "

"We *know* what you're doing," she said.

"What's that supposed to mean?" I asked.

Before she could answer, the first student then stood up. "The lying bitch doesn't know me. She's always accusing others of knowing more than they do. Meanwhile she continues to write in her stupid notebooks . . . page after page of the same thing, over and over."

"At least I don't lick toilets!" she said.

I stood up and walked closer to my class. "That's enough. This argument is not appropriate. Not in my class."

Both students looked at me with blank expressions. Perhaps they were used to instructors reprimanding them, and perhaps they just didn't care. But, to my relief, they both kept silent until the end of class.

I was sitting in my office reading when Dawn walked up to the doorway. "May I come in?" she asked.

"Of course."

She sat down across from me. "I heard you had quite a first class."

"Oh?"

"Jen and Kevin gave you some trouble?"

"Oh, yeah, those two. No, not much trouble. I expected there would be some adjusting to a new instructor."

"Yeah, but Kevin rarely ever speaks to the staff. Even his counselors."

"Should I feel honored?"

Dawn shook her head. "I wouldn't be. He's one you're going to have to keep an eye on."

It was during the last class of the week that I found out what Dawn had meant about Kevin.

I was almost done with my lecture when he raised his hand.

"Yes, Kevin?"

"May I stand up?"

"I don't see why not."

"Can I?"

"Yes, Kevin. You may stand up."

He stood up and waved his arms around. "All of this. Every single thing is contributing to my panic, to my masochism, my symptoms, and probably even the disease itself."

"We can't blow things out of proportion, Kevin. Your treatment, not to mention these classes, well, they are probably the best of the best in terms of rehabilitation."

"I don't know if that's true. I hear what you're saying, but I'm just not sure how it's going to affect my panic."

"You're letting your panic determine how you comprehend my words? Do you think that's going to work in your favor, Kevin?"

"Not in my favor, no, but maybe in a way that will decrease the symptoms or perhaps diminish the power of the disease."

"The disease is really not the issue here. It's not what's at stake."

"I don't know if that's true. I hear what you're saying, but I'm just not sure how it's going to affect my panic."

"You already said that, Kevin."

"I did?"

"Yes."

"But you don't believe me?"

"There's nothing to believe or disbelieve, Kevin. But I have to get back to teaching . . ."

"Wait! Is my panic causing a disruption? Do you want me to leave? Are you going to have me forcibly removed?"

"Where did you get that idea?"

"I can see it on your face. My panic is causing you stress."

"No, Kevin, I can assure you I am not stressed because of you. I'm here to help."

"I don't know if that's true. I hear what you're saying, but I'm just not sure how it's going to affect my panic."

"You just said it again, Kevin."

"Said what?"

"You know what."

"No, really, I don't. What did I say again?"

"I'm not here to play games, Kevin."

"This is not a game!"

"Please lower your voice."

"This is not a game."

"I know it's not, Kevin. Let's just have a seat and we can discuss this after class."

"This isn't working out for me."

"What isn't?"

"This room."

"Haven't you always had your classes in this room?"

"No. We usually had our classes in the basement."

"That's strange," I said, looking at the other students to gauge their reaction. They gave me nothing. They just stared.

"And now my panic is setting in deeper," Kevin said. "Should I recite one of your lessons? Will that help? Should I dig out my notes?"

"I think we will be ending class early."

"This is not a game!"

Jen turned to Kevin and said, "I think you need some new medication."

"I'm *on* medication. I'm always on medication."

"Well, it sure isn't helping," she said.

Kevin leaned in until he was inches from Jen's face. "This is not a game!"

I sat in my office. I thought about Kevin. I thought about what he had said.

This is not a game!

What did he mean by that?

I took out my pills and took two instead of just one.

I knew it wasn't a game.

Nothing was a game.

I hated games.

There was a knock on my door.

"Yes?" I asked.

"Can I come in?"

"Who is it?"

"Kevin."

"What?"

"Kevin."

"Come in."

Kevin walked in. He didn't look like himself, or rather, he didn't look like he had the last time I had seen him. His hair was shorter, and he was chubbier.

"Are you okay?" I asked.

"Yeah. Why?"

"You look . . . different."

"So do you."

"Do I?"

"Yeah."

He was staring at me. He was smiling. Why was he smiling?

"Do you need something?"

"Yeah."

"What?"

"Dawn said you could help me."

"Help you with what?"

"With my problems."

"This isn't usually how it's done."

"How is it done?"

"You have to go through the proper channels."

"I wasn't aware there were any."

"I'm sure someone went over the correct procedure with you when you came here, Kevin."

"Maybe. I don't remember."

"Do you have memory problems?"

"Sometimes."

"Is that one of your problems, Kevin?"

"Not really. I don't consider it a problem."

"Oh?"

"It's just something I have to live with."

"So what is it you need help with?"

"My panic."

"Panic?"

"Yeah."

"I think the other staff here is more equipped to handle panic attacks. I'm just an instructor."

"I'm not talking about panic attacks."

"Then what are you talking about?"

"Panic. In general. My panic, yeah, but also the panic I bring on others."

"What do you mean?"

"Whenever I'm around, people panic."

"Really?"

"Yeah."

"I'm not panicking."

"You will be. Always happens."

"I haven't heard any evidence of this . . . in class, I mean."

"Panic isn't always visible. Most panic is on the inside, you know."

"Kevin, is this some sort of trick you're playing on me?" I said, thankful that I avoided using the word *game*.

"No."

"I'm not sure what you need help in. Can we go get a counselor?"

"I don't need a counselor."

"Oh?"

"Counselors can't help. They panic the most, actually."

"Really, Kevin, this is getting us nowhere."

"How many pills did you take?"

"Excuse me?"

"You heard me. How many pills did you take? Does anyone know you are taking those? Does anyone know what they are? The side effects? The dosage? Do you have a prescription?"

"Kevin, this is inappropriate. I'm going to have to ask you to leave."

"Go ahead and ask, then."

"Please leave."

"That was a command, not a question."

"Would you please leave, Kevin?"

"That's better. But I still need your help."

"I can't help you."

"Really?"

"I can't."

"Must be the pills."

"Totally inappropriate, Kevin."

"Is it?"

"Yes."

"You still didn't tell me how many pills you took."

"Stop playing games, Kevin." I cursed myself for using that damn word.

"This is not a game!"

When Kevin left my office, I did not have the energy to do anything. My stomach hurt (as always), and my eyes were getting blurry. I swallowed another pill and worked on a jigsaw puzzle. Piece after piece after piece. It took me several hours, but I finished it.

I stared at the picture I had constructed. Three kittens playing with a ball of yarn. Grey kittens. Grey kittens in a cave.

I pushed the puzzle to the ground and let the pieces scatter. The kittens' eyes stayed intact, though, and they stared up at me. I knew I shouldn't have put the puzzle together. I was never able to handle puzzles. Puzzles are the worst for me, especially when I am on my medication.

The Taborica wasn't adjusting correctly.

I decided I had to take another.

Everything will be okay, I thought. *Everything will be just fine as long as Kevin got the help he needed.*

There was another knock on the door, but I ignored it. I wasn't going to let another person come in and disturb me, disturb my thought patterns and cause me to put together another jigsaw puzzle. I was never able to handle puzzles. Puzzles are the worst for me.

The person knocked again. I didn't answer. I wasn't going to say a word. I was just going to sit in my small office and wait for them to go away. I wasn't due in another class for a few hours. I had time. I had lots of time to just sit there and reflect on things, try to figure out what Kevin had been talking about.

What had he been talking about?

It's always like that, really. I go to a new place and get sucked into someone else's problems. He said he needed help, yes, but I was not sure that was the case. I think I am the one who might have needed the help. I'm not saying he was ever dangerous, but I might just be the one who would have needed things.

Things.

What things?

I had no idea.

I still don't, really.

What did I mean by *things?*

There is no real solution to any of the problems.

The grey kittens were still looking up at me as I ignored the knocking. The knocking continued for hours. I just sat there and ignored it while staring into the eyes of the kittens and trying to imagine myself in the cave along with them. I was in a cave, all alone, all alone to hibernate and hallucinate and contemplate my exposure to panic and all the things in that place. All the things that would destroy me, maybe. Just maybe.

Why did I take this job? What did I want?

Destruction wasn't what I wanted, no.

I needed help, wanted help. So did Kevin, right?

But I had failed him.

I shook my bottle and realized I only had one pill left.

I wasn't due for another refill for a week. What would I do? I didn't know. I thought about how great it would be if I could somehow clone the pill. Was there a machine that could turn one pill into several? I wanted there to be such a machine.

I thought about crushing the pill into dust and snorting it but that seemed too extreme, and I wasn't sure how my body would handle it. I would just have to hold onto the pill. I would have to have self-control. Self-control.

Self.

Control.

In the bathroom, I spent fifteen minutes reading the graffiti on the stall walls. I was surprised the administration didn't have the maintenance crew clean it off. The words were vulgar and cryptic, hinting at things I didn't understand, things I'm sure most people didn't understand. It fascinated me, though. Several people had taken the time to write on the walls while they sat on the toilet. The words they wrote did not appear random but seemed to display some level of premeditation.

It fascinated me.

It made me want to bring a pen or pencil into the bathroom and write something. Of course, I knew I couldn't bring myself to do that. That would be vandalism, and I wasn't a vandal.

I planned on bringing a small notebook with me to copy the words written on the bathroom stalls. I thought the words were important in some way. Yes, they held some significance to someone somewhere. I thought that maybe Kevin wrote all those words. Yes, Kevin might have written them in anticipation of my arrival. He had planned on my reading those words, obsessing over them, fantasizing about their importance.

Well played, Kevin. That's what I thought. You play the game well, Kevin.

"This is not a game!" I screamed.

They weren't listening to me. They never listened to me. I slammed my fist on the table and walked out of the room.

That was another thing I disliked about the Drake clinic. The people didn't really listen to you. They just pretended. They'd stare at you, nod their heads, even respond to you a little bit but they never really listened. They never attempted to comprehend what I said. The administration was an untouchable entity that a person *could not* reason with. My questions and concerns were left ignored day after day.

As I sat in my office, I started talking to myself, leading myself into a labyrinth of inner talk full of dirty revelations and paranoid accusations. I know myself best. That's one thing I do know. I know myself so well and cannot help but lead myself into secrets.

Someone knocked on my door. I told them to go away but they kept knocking. Finally, I opened the door only to see Mr. Caudal, the head of the clinic, standing in the hall-way.

"Mr. L——?" he said.

"What?"

"Is everything okay?"

"Yes. Why?"

"You didn't answer the door when I knocked."

"I just answered."

"Can we go to my office and talk?"

"No. No, I can't do that." I didn't want to go. I didn't want to discuss things on their time schedule. They wanted to leave me powerless.

"I have to insist we do so."

"Why? I don't see any reason for that."

"Come on. Follow me."

I didn't move. My breathing became labored. I was suffocating right there in the doorway.

"Do you want me to leave?" I asked. "Are you going to have me forcibly removed?"

"Where did you get that idea?"

"I can see it on your face. I'm causing you stress."

"No, Mr. L——, I can assure you I am not stressed out, especially as a result of you. I'm here to help."

"I don't know if that's true. I hear what you're saying, but I'm just not sure how it's going to affect my . . . my panic."

"Let's go."

"No!"

"I'm not here to play games, Mr. L——."

"This is not a game!"

"Please lower your voice."

"This is not a game."

"I know it's not. Let's just go to my office and we can discuss this."

"This isn't working out for me."

"What isn't?"

"This place."

"Didn't you make the choice to come here?"

"I don't remember. One day I just woke up, and I was here."

"That's absurd," he said. "I don't think you know what you're saying."

"I know everything I'm saying."

"Stop playing games."

"This is not a game!"

I did go to Mr. Caudal's office, and we did talk. He gave me a puzzle to put together. I imagine it was some sort of aptitude test. Piece after piece after piece. It took me several hours, but I finished it.

I stared at the picture I had constructed. Three kittens playing with a ball of yarn. Grey kittens. Grey kittens in a cave.

I pushed the puzzle to the ground and let the pieces scatter. The kittens' eyes stayed intact and stared up at me. I knew I shouldn't have put the puzzle together. I was never able to handle puzzles. Puzzles are the worst for me, especially when I am on my medication.

And I am always on medication.

Notes on a Horror

By Dr. Raymond Thoss

I WILL call myself Dr. Thoss. I am a clinical psychologist who works principally with child trauma. I have worked extensively with adult trauma as well, primarily because most of what we know about treating trauma began with adults and then was modified for children. The first documented and successful case of prosecuted child abuse was that of little Mary Ellen Wilson, a 10-year-old girl, in 1875.[1] This was not prosecuted under civil rights law or criminal law. It was prosecuted under animal cruelty law. It's wrong to beat your livestock. Children are livestock. Ergo, it's wrong to beat your child. See. Logic. Progress. It wasn't until 1961 that C. Henry Kempe coined the term "battered-child syndrome," which we now know as physical abuse.[2] It wasn't until 1998 that Vincent Felitti and his team at Kaiser Permanente, while looking at why people could not lose weight, found out that many of his patients were overeating due to, for

---

[1] Robert W. ten Bensel, Marguerite M. Rheinberger, and Samuel X. Radbill, "Children in a World of Violence: The Roots of Child Maltreatment," in *The Battered Child*, 5th Edition, ed. Mary Edna Helfer, Ruth S. Kempe, and Richard D. Krugman (Chicago: The University of Chicago Press, 1997), 3-28.

[2] Ibid.

example, child sexual abuse. He found that more than half of his almost twenty-thousand-person sample reported an "Adverse Childhood Experience" (ACE), such as:

1) Child physical abuse
2) Child sexual abuse
3) Child emotional abuse
4) Parental drug use
5) Loss of a parent for any reason (e.g., death or parent leaving)
6) Severe mental illness of a parent
7) Parent incarcerated
8) Domestic violence in the household[3]

He found that one ACE made a person 80% more likely to have another ACE and that there were significant health impacts associated with having them. A person with an ACE score of 4 was 390% more likely to develop chronic obstructive pulmonary disease (COPD). A male with an ACE score of 6 or higher was 4600% more likely to be an IV drug user. Psychology research is used to small rates; a ten percent decrease in depressive symptoms is significant. But these rates were astronomical. Now . . . now we knew that child trauma is a legitimate issue.[4]

The first child I ever worked with who had trauma embodied all the points raised in the extensive child trauma literature, in an actual

---

[3] Vincent J. Felitti, et al., "Relationship of Childhood Abuse and Household Dysfunction to Many of the Leading Causes of Death in Adults: The Adverse Childhood Experience (ACE) Study," *American Journal of Preventative Medicine* 14 (1998), 245-258. These are the eight ACEs of the original study. Since then Felitti and his team have added two more, child physical neglect and child emotional neglect. When I speak of ACEs beginning from Section 1, I will be speaking of all ten of them when I refer to them as a group.

[4] The ACE study is now housed in the Center for Disease Control (CDC) to reflect that although ACEs are not a "mental health" problem, they are, as Dr. Robert Block (former President of the American Academy of Pediatrics) has said, "the greatest unaddressed public health threat of our time." See https://www.cdc.gov/violenceprevention/acestudy.

human being standing in front of me. Sixteen-year-old Hispanic male. Multiple, multiple ACEs. I met him when he was sixteen. He said the worst thing that ever happened to him, out of a lifetime of horrible things, was when he was eight. Late. Driving home from dinner. Pickup truck, single cab, whole family in a line, like ducks in a shooting gallery. Dad driving, Mom in the middle, he was near the passenger door. Dad was on some really good stuff. Dad wanted to kill his mother. As the young man tells me, "He was really aiming for her. I was just in the way." Dad opens the door while they are going 60 on the highway headed home. Dad tries to push mom out the truck. The boy clings on to his mother so he doesn't fall out of a speeding vehicle on the highway at 60 mph. He says, "I saw a 'black river', then we were home." We will talk about this when we discuss dissociation. This is the way trauma impacts memory formation. He "lost" time. He says, "I tumbled out of the truck." He turned. Dad pinned mom to the bed of the truck, hands around her neck. The boy was eight. Dad was two-hundred fifteen pounds and on drugs. The boy fought. The boy couldn't win. He ran into the house. He told his sixteen-year-old brother, "Dad is killing mom!" Brother and brother's friends ran out. By that time dad was gone. Mom was gagging but semi-conscious. And here is where he tells me the thing I can't forget. Ever.

"Everyone was looking at my mom. My brother and his friends. I looked for a second. She was okay. She was breathing. But when I knew she was okay, I looked behind the truck, toward the park near our house. And I saw it. It was my dad, running into the darkness. He looked like a shadow, like a monster. And that's been my whole life. Everyone else looks away from the darkness. Me, though, that's my whole life, looking *right into* the darkness. The Darkness, I'll always be looking into the Darkness." I've never forgotten that.

This article is a conversation about the Darkness and how Thomas Ligotti helped me navigate myself and my children through it.

Section 1: Ontological Gaslighting

A few points of clarification. First, I am (obviously, I hope) using a pseudonym. My opinions, the opinions I am about to describe to you, are "not mainstream" at best and "dangerous" at worst. You may guess why this is once you've heard them. Second, if you take away one thing from this article, it should be this: Trauma Disconnects; Healing Re-connects. If you take away two things from this article, they should be: Trauma survives and persists by being INVISIBLE. This is why I consider child abuse an apolitical issue. Ask the staunchest red Republican or the staunchest blue Democrat this question: "Do you care if children get raped?" They will answer, of course. Now the cynic in me says neither of them really cares, and that may be true, but there is a much deeper obstacle. Child abuse is still not "real" to them when they are asked this question. And here we come to the first intersection, what I call "ontological gaslighting."

In existentialist philosophy, Heidegger speaks of the guttural, authentic reality of Death versus the abstract, inauthentic "reality" of death.[1] The existentialist example is inauthentic ("Hey, smoking could kill you,") vs. the authentic ("Mr. Smith, we have found multiple malignant tumors in your lungs. You have approximately six months to live.") Knowing about child abuse and *knowing* about child abuse exist on inauthentic and authentic levels. So long as the knowledge stays on the inauthentic level, it remains invisible. So long as it is invisible, it will perpetuate. Asking "Do you care if children get raped?" is a different level of authenticity than, "Hey. See that 6-year-old boy? He was raped. He's in your office. What will you do for him?" Thomas Ligotti most eloquently describes this

---

[1] Martin Heidegger, *Being and Time* (New York: Harper Collins, 1963).

invisibility brought about by inauthenticity throughout his story, "In the Shadow of Another World," and most specifically in its final lines:

> How can they know what it is their houses are truly nestled among? They cannot see, nor even wish to see, that world of shadows with which they consort every moment of their brief and innocent lives. But often, perhaps during the visionary time of twilight, I am sure they have sensed it.

People do not see it. Cannot? Do not wish to? Whichever it is, it is irrelevant. It is not the seeing or not seeing that matters. It is this "time of twilight" that you will be witness to as I take you through this phenomenon of child abuse. It is this "time of twilight" my children have seen. The easiest and clearest way I know to do this is to take you through a typical day at my job. The purpose of this is to highlight the intersections of child abuse and several topics that are common themes, constructs, and sources of Ligottian literature. I first encountered Thomas Ligotti at the age of seventeen. There are, of course, therapists who work with child abuse who have no abuse history themselves. However, the ACE study demonstrates that child trauma is the norm, not the exception, so there are of course those of us who have their own trauma history and who work with child abuse victims for a deeply personal reason founded in this. I myself have all the ACEs but one – nine total. I have seen therapists with ACEs who are great therapists. I have seen therapists without any ACE who are great therapists. I have seen therapists with ACEs who are awful therapists. I have seen therapists without ACEs who are awful therapists. My personal observation is that therapists with ACEs who are effective therapists have done their own work prior to, or concurrent with, this job. Never use the job as therapy for yourself. That is a disservice to both you and the children we serve.

When I encountered Ligotti at age seventeen, I was deeply suicidal, as directly related to twelve years of ongoing child abuse and other traumas (such as the death of people I loved). Thomas Ligotti gave the most beautiful eloquence to things I saw but no one else would ever affirm. It resonated with my reality and the reality of those who were like me. To encapsulate in a single sentence what Thomas Ligotti did for me: He literally saved my life. When everyone else, therapists included, told me I was "depressed" or "mentally ill," he told me, "No. You are not. You are awake." As I went through the work I needed to do prior to being a doctor to these children, I read everything published by Ligotti. And I saw deep connections between the world of child abuse (my world and my patients' world) and the world Thomas Ligotti described. It is this worldview that he calls the Conspiracy against the Human Race. I had personally coined the term "ontological gaslighting" to refer to it, defined as the recognition that existence itself is insane and that when you witness this insanity—as my clients who have been abused witnessed it, as the protagonist in "In the Shadow of Another World" and other Ligottian protagonists witnessed it, as I, myself, witnessed it—you, yourself, feel an insanity due to the fact of no one believing that you are surrounded by insanity. Should you try to convince them the world is insane, their response is simple: *You* are insane. They do not believe that *they* are surrounded by insanity. Maybe they cannot believe this. According to *The Conspiracy Against the Human Race*[2] and the Norwegian philosopher Peter Wessel Zapffe, there is a type of hardwired evolutionary and metaphysical inclination *not* to believe this.

The ACE study contradicts the "typical" view (i.e., that the world is not fundamentally insane). Empirically what is demonstrated through the ACE study is that trauma is not the

---

[2] When *TCATHR* is in italics, it will denote the work published by Thomas Ligotti in 2010. When TCATHR is referred to without italics, it will refer to the abstract concept.

exception. It's the norm. It therefore contradicts the "typical" view. When more than half the population has experienced something, it is, by definition, "normal." However, existence itself conspires to the effect that people do not see reality as insane (a reality where children are abused every ten seconds in the US), but we who have suffered this insanity *must* be insane.[3] For if we are not, then the only alternative left is that reality itself is a type of insanity and horror. This is unacceptable to the majority, to the status quo. I believe this is not intentional by most people. It is how Being itself persists, how our species persists according to Ligotti and Zapffe. Ligotti incisively interprets Zapffe on this point: "As Zapffe concluded, we need to hamper our consciousness for all we are worth, or it will impose upon us a too clear vision of what we do not want to see."[4] This would result in the demonstration of Being as an ultimate nightmare, thus ceasing the persistence of our species, thus ceasing the persistence of Being. In other words, Being itself "gaslights" us who have directly borne witness to the insanity, to trauma, as is seen by the residents of "In the Shadow of Another World" and other Ligottian protagonists who bear witness to the sheer insanity and horror of existence. For if Being did not "ontologically gaslight" us, Being would not persist.

Thomas Ligotti's expression of this worldview is uniquely and eloquently his own. But the view itself, the visionary time of twilight, I believe to be ubiquitous in child trauma among both those of us who work in the field and those of us who have survived childhood trauma. This is one of my purposes for this article: to connect the expression of the Ligottian view to the reality of child trauma. There is, of course, an ulterior motive. I believe I have become a better

---

[3] "Child Abuse Statistics & Facts," *Childhelp*, accessed August 15, 2016, https://www.childhelp.org/child-abuse-statistics.

[4] Thomas Ligotti, *The Conspiracy Against the Human Race* (New York: Hippocampus Press, 2010), 27.

psychologist for the children I serve because of Thomas Ligotti. Not only did he save my life, but I use his writings daily to save other lives.

So, what is a day like? How about Monday? Let's start there.

Section 2: Ubiquity of Iniquity and Gnostic Disconnect

I arrive in the office to return phone calls from the weekend. A sixty-five-year-old woman has left me a message. Our center works primarily with those eighteen and under, as we are technically a child trauma clinic. Our goal is to expand our age range, for obvious reasons. I return her call and this woman talks about having seen every therapist in the community, and that none understood her. This woman, like many children I work with, has no "before." People often assume that for individuals who have undergone trauma there was a "before the trauma." Many of my children do not have this. This is the only thing they have ever known; trauma is literally the only reality for them. This woman is the sixty-five-year-old version of my children. No before. As she speaks of decades of trauma, starting from as far back as she can remember, an image that has popped in my mind many times when I have had similar conversations with patients occurs again. The Stranger. Not Camus, although not irrelevant. Go farther back. Gnostics. Their image of the Stranger, the Alien.

> In the world of darkness I dwelt thousands of myriads of years and nobody knew of me that I was there. . . . Year upon year and generation upon generation I was there, and they did not know about me that I dwelt in their world.[5]

This is as accurate a description of this woman's decades of abuse

---

[5] Hans Jonas, *The Gnostic Religion* (Boston: Beacon Press, 1963), 54.

and trauma, particularly the disconnection that trauma brings, the utter existential and visceral loneliness, as anyone could hope for. This relates to the point I made in section 1, that trauma is invisible; ergo, there is no problem because out of sight, out of mind. Similar to the previous quote, the concept of the Stranger implies alienation, loneliness, and a dark outcome to self-awareness. This connects with what Zapffe calls "a damning surplus of consciousness."[6] The Gnostics can be interpreted claiming that the role of the Stranger serves a very important function for this "damning surplus." "In his alienation from himself the distress is gone," writes Jonas, "but this very fact is the culmination of the Stranger's tragedy."[7] To survive, the Stranger must disconnect from him/herself. The philosopher Hannah Arendt describes this phenomenon as "loneliness" and distinguishes it from mere solitude. She states, "Solitude can become loneliness; this happens when all by myself I am deserted by my own self."[8] This alienation, this role of the Stranger's alienation from himself (it is argued from this synthesis), is to ease the "damning surplus of consciousness." This is what I see with this sixty-five-year-old woman – a woman so fractured by life's evils that she must, to survive, "desert" herself, disconnect from herself at a fundamental level, so that she can function in a world that denies the very existence of her experiences.

Inherent in the Gnostic view is that the world is fundamentally "evil." I will continue to use this word despite its protean shape and plethora of interpretations. It is foundational to the world as described by my patients and by this woman. Perhaps "evil" is too nebulous a term. Shattered may be closer. Trauma disconnects,

---

[6] Thomas Ligotti, *The Conspiracy Against the Human Race* (New York: Hippocampus Press, 2010), 23.

[7] Jonas, *The Gnostic Religion*, 50.

[8] Hannah Arendt, *The Origins of Totalitarianism* (New York: Harcourt Brace and Company, 1976), 476.

healing reconnects. There are two fundamental misunderstandings I typically see from people who are encountering this field for the first time. The first I will discuss in this section. The second I will discuss in the next section.

The first (and perhaps the most profound, because it is so closely related to the ontological gaslighting described previously) is that by not actively refuting that the world is evil, we automatically agree, automatically give consent, to that interpretation. No. We, as healers, as guides, do *not* condone the shattered world; we simply bear witness. A simplistic definition of empathy that I teach my trainees is that empathy is not standing above a person in a dark hole and offering advice; empathy is taking a ladder, climbing down that hole, and sitting beside the person. Bearing witness does not automatically imply condoning what one is witnessing

Simply put, therapists do not see the world as evil and this detracts from our ability to help our patients because we are not closer to our patients if we cannot, at the very least, entertain the idea of the world as evil. This requires more explanation. If you allow yourself to admit the world as evil, as inherently shattered, then you are closer to your patient because effective therapeutic interactions are founded on building and maintaining a relationship (even the relatively historically recent movement known as Evidence-Based Practice in Psychology emphasizes the importance of a therapeutic relationship). Relationships, at minimum, require empathy, perspective-taking of the other's viewpoint (climbing down that hole). The less this occurs, the farther you are from that person; the more you can do this, the closer you are to that person. If you are closer to your patient, you are better able to help them. This does not *condone* the shattered world. It just validates it, recognizes it, and *empathizes* with the world they see. We cannot pass to a possibility of a world as not evil[9] until we validate the world as evil. I would argue that the most important aspect of this phone call from a sixty-five-year-old woman is that I validate that her world exists, that what she sees is real, that she is seeing/experiencing something *actual*. How can we ever hope to get to the neighborhood of anything approaching help if we outright dismiss that worldview?

For some patients, this inability to have another person, especially a professional, validate this worldview is the most significant barrier. This was, in effect, what this woman told me: Everyone tried to "get me better" but never began with a validation of her worldview. Medication, cognitive processing therapy (CPT), eye movement desensitization and reprocessing (EMDR)—nothing worked the way she was promised. None met her in *her* world; all started in another world, a world where "All things happen for a reason," a world where "It'll be all right." The world she inhabits has no reason. It is not, nor will it be, all right. This sixty-five-year-old woman has spent the last sixty-five years tortured. What reason is there for that? How is that all right? There is a freedom and a very specific type of dark hope and comfort in the type of nihilism that Thomas Ligotti describes.

> All will be dulled in the power of your vision, which will give you to see that the greatest power, the only power, is to care for nothing.[10]

This is a powerful lesson from Ligotti's writings. It is a gross misinterpretation that he would condone, that is, agree and/or

---

[9] Should that be a choice we wish to make. The choice is not mandatory or obligatory.

[10] Thomas Ligotti, *Songs of a Dead Dreamer* (New York: Carroll & Graf, 1990), 180.

acquiesce to, the suffering and horror of the world. As an example, in the philosophical view of antinatalism, there is no condoning of the world as evil, no assertion that it is "all right" that the world is evil. There is simply an acknowledgment of the world as such and a potential response to this situation.[11] The crucial point is that to have *any* response to the reality of the world as evil one must *first acknowledge it as such*. The responses "All things happen for a reason" or "It'll be all right" present no such acknowledgment. In fact, they present the exact opposite: a dismissal. Therefore, any response that begins with such a dismissal, no matter the number of randomized controlled trials, can have no coherent or effective response to an individual who inhabits the world described by Thomas Ligotti, the world inhabited by this sixty-five-year-old woman, a world where individuals are not insane, but the very world itself is.

This acknowledgement is the core starting point for any effective reconnection, healing, or guidance for a patient. In essence, a desire to hold onto the world as "good" closes the admission of other possibilities or interpretations, and this is deeply problematic as a core component of reconnection is reinterpretation.[12] This starting point is presented in no therapeutic manual. The intellectually generous response is that these manuals or approaches assume this acknowledgment. A less generous response is that this starting point is simply not thought of. So this is what I did for the woman. "Yes, your world is bad. You are not crazy. You are awake." I did what Thomas Ligotti did for me when

---

[11] David Benatar, *Better Never to Have Been: The Harm of Coming Into Existence* (Oxford: Oxford University Press, 2006).

[12] Reinterpretation or "reframing" is a core and critical component of most cognitive-behavioral therapies (see Judith S. Beck, *Cognitive Behavior Therapy*, 2nd ed., New York: The Guilford Press, 2011), especially for traumatic stress. Without reinterpretation (or, more specifically, with the automatic closing off of certain "forbidden" interpretations), one has significantly decreased the power of this core, critical component.

I was seventeen. That's where I learned to do this. In its essence, this acknowledgment is an acknowledgment that you are no longer asleep – you are awake. The responses "All things happen for a reason" and "It'll be all right" are a soporific that tries to lull one back to sleep. I am agnostic toward the tactic of lulling one back to sleep. I personally hold no strong opinion either way.[13] From my clinical judgment, and from the outcome data on attempts to perform this with PTSD (e.g., medications are notoriously ineffective in treatment of PTSD as a front-line approach), I have not seen the soporific tactic as an effective approach. People can't get back to sleep. They are awake. Acknowledge this. And then we can move forward should they choose to. This leads into Section 3 and the second fundamental misunderstanding.

Section 3: The Shattered and the Tattered

I start the morning with consultation calls to therapists across the United States, therapists who are working with child abuse victims. I am a consultant in multiple evidence-based treatments for children and adolescents, and a key component to effective implementation and dissemination is to see, via consultation calls, how therapists implement a specific treatment. The therapist on the 10 a.m. call talks about a child they have who has completely shut down, completely *disconnected*, in the therapist's words. The child isn't angry or sad or scared. The child is numb. The child feels nothing. When the foster parent asked this child what was wrong one day, the child flatly responded, "I'm shattered."

This brings us to the second misunderstanding. The second misunderstanding is of the word "disconnection." People tend to interpret it narrowly, e.g., "Of course she is disconnected from her

---

[13] In fact, I believe that one does not necessarily "need to be fixed." After all, the world *is* insane.

emotions." No. That is too conservative. This disconnection is very real. I mean this on a fundamental level. The neuroscientist Antonio Damasio has written a lot of popular, as well as technical, pieces on exactly how ingrained connection is within the human organism. Dr. Damasio's work centers on this process of "normal" connection. It is instructive to compare this normal connection with the shattered connection that trauma, by definition, brings. Dr. Damasio speaks of how one's sense of self, what we refer to when we say the word "'I," is deeply connected to our physical sensations.[14] Dr. Bessel Van Der Kolk refers to this as "interoception," the awareness of our sensory, body-based feelings; as he says, "the greater the awareness of your body-based feelings, the greater your potential to control your life."[15] From neuroimaging studies, we know that people who suffer trauma tend to have their prefrontal cortex "turned off."[16] If you suffer more trauma, especially chronically and interpersonally over time, the brain "turns off" even more, to the point where only the most basic functions of respiration and blood flow are online. If you were to look at an fMRI scan of a person who suffered focal trauma (e.g., a car collision) and has PTSD, you would see the frontal lobe shut off but the amygdala (one of the key parts of the brain having to do with emotions) still lighting up. If you were to look at an fMRI scan of a person who had chronic, interpersonal trauma over many years (as with most of my kids), you would see a small light at the back of the scan indicating that respiration, blood flow, etc., are working, but not much else.[17] The first scan would look like a house with Christmas lights compared to the second. The second scan would look like a house in a Thomas Ligotti story. A single window with a

---

[14] Antonio Damasio, *The Feeling of What Happens* (New York: Harcourt, 1999).

[15] Bessel Van Der Kolk, *The Body Keeps the Score* (New York: Viking, 2014), 95.

[16] Ibid., 68-72.

[17] Ibid.

single candle. Nothing else. In psychology, we call this dissociation. Dissociation exists on a spectrum from the daydream variety (low level) to the chronic sense of depersonalization (high level). Neurologically, it is represented by the previously cited imaging studies. Your brain is literally shutting down, literally disconnecting. This is not simply a metaphor. It is fragmenting, disconnecting, on a neurological level. Scientifically this is what dissociation is.

However, this scientific explanation is dry, and although it is accurate, it lacks the power of true description. For phenomenological descriptions of dissociation, Thomas Ligotti has no peer. and his writings are punctuated with such descriptions of people disconnected from "reality," *dissociated* from "reality." The entirety of the works *In a Foreign Town, In a Foreign Land* and *This Degenerate Little Town* are phenomenological descriptions similar to what my clients who have severe dissociation suffer. Moreover, and attesting to the brilliance of Thomas Ligotti, not only are these works descriptions of what my clients suffer from, but they are descriptions of *why* they suffer from severe dissociation.

> "What Ascrobius sought," the doctor explained, "was not a remedy for his physical disease, not a cure in any usual sense of the word. What he sought was an absolute *annulment*, not only of his disease but of his entire existence. On rare occasions he even spoke to me," the doctor said, "about the uncreation of his whole life.[18]

> There are those among us
> who claim to have seen
> this degenerate little town,
> although they may be unaware
> of its true nature.

---

[18] Thomas Ligotti, *Teatro Grottesco* (London: Virgin, 2008), 123.

> There are those who have emerged
> from some painful ordeal
> of the body or of the mind
> and then begun speaking
> of how they saw in the distance
> an outline of crooked houses
> tilting this way and that,
> or walked along some twisted street
> and felt the ground soft with decay
> beneath their steps,
> or even glimpsed those diseased faces,
> their skin rough and pale as plaster,
> peeking from behind grimy windows.[19]

These passages may represent the best phenomenological descriptions of the disconnection and depersonalization alluded to by clinical, scientific descriptions of dissociation and why they occur (the desire to "uncreate" a life; "some painful ordeal"). However, dissociation can exist interpersonally as well, without the extremes of dissociation that we have been discussing. Remember, dissociation is on a spectrum; it is not categorical.

Ligotti, of course, has passages about this interpersonal disconnection. We discussed how the Stranger, in Gnostic literature, is also a prime example of this *dis*connection. At the same time, I would argue that Lovecraft's "The Outsider" is the best description of interpersonal dissociation, also known as alienation in common vernacular. For example: "Such a lot the gods gave me—to me, the dazed, the disappointed; the barren, the broken."[20] Lovecraft even uses the same concept as the Gnostics: "I know always that I am an

---

[19] Thomas Ligotti, *This Degenerate Little Town* (London: Durtro, 2001), 66.

[20] H.P. Lovecraft, *Tales* (New York: The Library of America, 2005), 8.

outsider; a stranger in this century and among those who are still men."[21] The protagonist does not even feel human. I have heard this same thing from more children than I can count at this point. This story is perhaps the best self-encapsulated piece of prose that captures interpersonal dissociation on a phenomenological level. It is what the children I work with feel every day.

Section 4: The Darkness . . . The Darkness

I close my day out by seeing my four individual clients for that day. A very light individual caseload. My previous assignments: forty hours, forty clients, and pray for a no-show so you can do your paperwork and billing. This is typical of the state of mental health service delivery in the public sector. Today it is two females, two males. All adolescents. With my female patients, we are in a part of treatment clumsily termed "cognitive processing." Clumsy because it can be a powerful tool when done properly and entirely ineffective when done incorrectly. As Kant demonstrated, we construct our world, we bring something to the world of experience that the world of experience doesn't have intrinsically. Cognitive processing is, to (over)simplify, reconstruction of one's world. Thus, it's also called "cognitive restructuring." It is, for all intents and purposes, relative to this conversation, identical to the concepts of "reframing" and reinterpretation we discussed earlier.

In my mind, each new interpretation, each new cognitive structure, is a new "world." I've always wondered how one could do this work if one purposely ignores potential worlds. In my experience, one is only as good at cognitive processing as the number of worlds one is willing to gaze upon, to admit exist. Thomas Ligotti, in my interpretation of his writings, has never encouraged one to "hate" the world, much less to harm others in

---

[21] Ibid., 14.

the world; the Conspiracy he speaks of merely argues that we ignore the world as it fundamentally is. Any value judgments are left to us and us alone. Thus, for me, this cognitive processing/restructuring is simply a process of presenting worlds and letting my patients choose from them. With one adolescent, I talk about a concept I have heard of as "a family of choice," the idea that "family" is not necessarily the biological family you grew up with, the biological family who hurt you. Instead, "family" is a membership you must earn. Ergo, "family" can be blood or not, friends or relatives or both. She resonates with this concept, with this world. It helps her to manage her feelings and thoughts toward a mother who never was a mother to her. However, the adolescent girl I see during the next hour rejects this concept. To her, family is blood and that is what family must be. This is also a valid choice. I never "fight" with my patients. After all, Thomas Ligotti never "fought" with me to accept his worldview. Additionally, although I experienced my own trauma, I do not know *their* specific phenomenological experience of trauma. So, I accept that one girl accepts this world of a "family of choice," and I accept that another girl rejects this world. To the one who rejects the world, I simply present a different one. And I continue this process until she finds one that suits her.

Implicit in offering these choices is that the Darkness is a completely valid perspective. My children have looked into the abyss, and the abyss has also looked into them. But they did not choose to look into it. They were witness to a nightmare that they never should have been witness to. And when they tell of what they've seen, they are dismissed, because others who have not seen the Darkness cannot believe that this is a fundament of the world. They cannot believe that the world is fundamentally insane. But Thomas Ligotti validated this for me. And in doing so, he quite literally saved my life. To deny this perspective is the Conspiracy he speaks of. It is a lethal conspiracy. All four children I see at the end of my Monday wanted to kill themselves prior to coming to me. *I* would have killed myself. I wanted to so badly, until Ligotti validated that "Yes, the Darkness is real. I will show you the shattered and tattered and broken world. A world of fragmented ubiquitous iniquity. You are not insane. The world is. You are simply awake."

This is what the first child I ever worked with who had trauma was told. When I saw the Darkness that night I could not comprehend what I witnessed. I saw a monster. For my father was the most evil human being I have ever met. He tortured my mother and me for years. And when he tried to kill us that night by throwing us out of that speeding truck, my world was utterly annihilated. When I was young, I inhaled the horror genre like how-to manuals. Romero taught me a shot to the head stops a lot of things. Lovecraft taught me the universe was indifferent to me and my plight. But it wasn't until I found Thomas Ligotti that I was validated in my view of the world as a place where a father tries to push his child out of a moving vehicle, a place where he beats his wife daily. A place where, although most parents would say to their child, every day, "I love you," he told me, "I wish you were never born." The Conspiracy dictated to "well-intentioned" people that the most "mentally healthy" thing they could do was to say I was depressed, or to medicate me. For to do otherwise would be to shatter the Conspiracy, and that cannot stand in a sane world.

This is one of the gifts I bring to my patients that I first learned from Thomas Ligotti: I bring a world where their phenomenological and experiential data is validated, not dismissed. I bring a world where the priority is not to sustain the illusion of a sane world, to sustain the Conspiracy, but to bear witness to the metaphysical insanity that has constituted most, if not all, of their lives. My personal hope is that they will move beyond this world, for I've also discovered that there are an infinite number of worlds. Once you have stared upon the destruction and annihilation of your own world, and only after you have truly looked at the horror, truly born witness, you can turn your gaze to the infinity of worlds surrounding you, should that be a choice you wish to make. But to tell one to ignore the annihilation, or that the annihilation never happened, is not only dismissive, it is disrespectful to the experience the person brings. It is inhumane. I chose to turn my gaze elsewhere after bearing witness. Others do not. Either is a completely valid choice with no value judgment placed on it. At the same time, I know I could not have made the choice to turn my gaze to other worlds unless Thomas Ligotti had given me the conceptual apparatus and language to express the utter annihilation of my world. He wrote a song about a dead world, a world I knew, and the song brought tears to me. But when the song was done, so were the tears. And I knew I could move forward if I chose. The fact that Thomas Ligotti did not mandate or demand that I move forward made it possible for me to do so.

Thomas Ligotti. He saved my life with his song. I use his song to save others' lives. For this, I thank him. For this, others thank him. And with this, my day is completed.

Bibliography

Arendt, Hannah. *The Origins of Totalitarianism*. New York: Harcourt Brace and Company, 1976.

Beck, Judith S. *Cognitive Behavior Therapy*. 2nded. New York: The Guilford Press, 2011.

Benatar, David. *Better Never to Have Been: The Harm of Coming Into Existence*. Oxford: Oxford University Press, 2006.

"Child Abuse Statistics and Facts." *Child Help*. Accessed August 15, 2016. https://www.childhelp.org/child-abuse-statistics.

Damasio, Antonio. *The Feeling of What Happens*. New York: Harcourt, 1999.

Felitti, Vincent J., et al. "Relationship of Childhood Abuse and Household Dysfunction to Many of the Leading Causes of Death in Adults: The Adverse Childhood Experience (ACE) Study." *American Journal of Preventative Medicine* 14, no. 4 (1998): 245-258.

Heidegger, Martin. *Being and Time*. New York: Harper Collins, 1963.

Jonas, Hans. *The Gnostic Religion*. Boston: Beacon Press, 1963.

Ligotti, Thomas. *The Conspiracy Against the Human Race*. New York: Hippocampus Press, 2010.

———. *Songs of a Dead Dreamer*. New York: Carroll & Graf, 1990.

———. *Teatro Grottesco*. London: Virgin, 2008.

———. *This Degenerate Little Town*. London: Durtro, 2001.

Lovecraft, H.P. *Tales*. New York: The Library of America, 2005.

ten Bensel, Robert W., Marguerite M. Rheinberger, and Samuel X. Radbill. "Children in a World of Violence: The Roots of Child Maltreatment." In *The Battered Child*, 3-28. 5th ed. Edited by Mary Edna Helfer, Ruth S. Kempe, and Richard D. Krugman. Chicago: The University of Chicago Press, 1997.

Van Der Kolk, Bessel. *The Body Keeps the Score*. New York: Viking, 2014.

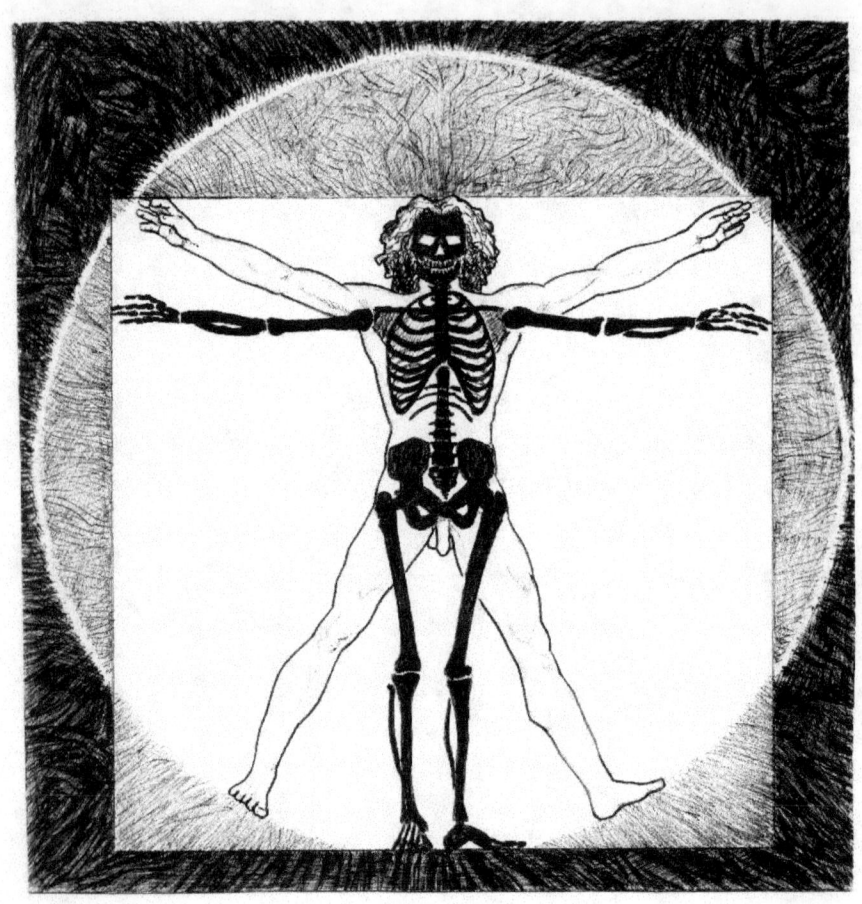

Title: Black Universe
Artist: Dejan Ognjanović

Singing the Song of My Unmaking

By Christopher Ropes

I.

Layer by layer, the world flakes away,
its insides withdrawing in flight from the
cancerous decay.
The light peels off and is blown on
a wind that consumes itself, leaving stillness.
The love flickers and fades and lets fly
a howl of defeat and a whimper of surrender
before cooling to embers, then to ash.

I strip off my clothes, mutilate my naked body
with hands and knives, knives for hands,
and I coat myself with the ashes, stumble
out of my bedroom prison and wait to become ash.
A pile of me at one with my mourning shroud,

not even stirred by a gentle breeze,
because this impossible world has
divided itself by zero, and nothing survives the absurdity.

II.

Depression is a philosophy of active nihilism. It is not content to accept passively that all is ultimately meaningless. It must engage the meaningless world in an internal analysis and negate it. All things are weighed and measured and found wanting. Depression is not merely an illness, a bogeyman mental disease. It is a philosophy, as I said, a theology, a lifestyle that was not chosen, a chewing the world up and spitting it out in disgust and queasiness.

I am not afflicted with depression. I am not a victim. I do not suffer from depression. I am depression. You're not supposed to identify so closely with your illness, the doctors and therapists tell you, but how do you not when depression is flesh of your flesh? My bones are the dust of a dead civilization. My hands fold in prayer to a thirsting void, and my blood is the void's tears. I have made two serious attempts on my own life. And I have spent many a lonesome night too broken to even close the book of my life, too tired, too spiteful to give life the pleasure of having crushed me.

Ligotti is right. Suicide is a life-affirming act. There are places in the mind where the world and its people and pleasures are so far away, they seem to be puppets of nonexistence, imaginary, unreality given the faintest of forms. And the idea of suicide in those dark places is a joke. Let's laugh at how pointless it would be. Why lash out against life? Life will grin mockery right back at you if you do. Life, even when it takes the form of death, always wins.

Apathy is the true opposite of love, some say. My suicide attempts were a dance with life, a hateful romance with my tormentor. A Ligotti story, and I was the one seeking the secret book, the forbidden tome promising a glimpse of the merciless

Truth. In the demilitarized zones beyond the suicidal, life is that ex-lover you only think about when you see yourself in an ancient photograph with him or her, and you realize you can't remember their voice. You shrug. You move on.

I've spent years at each level.

My first suicide attempt was the night before my nineteenth birthday. August 16th, 1991. I took a bunch of pills, burned holes in my stomach, was taken to the hospital vomiting blood. My mom called at 3:23 AM, the precise time of my birth, the precise time when I heard my EMT cousin's scanner screech out that an ambulance and police were on their way to where I lived. I picked up the phone, the phone that leered at me in the knowledge that it could cause me so much hurt. I said, "Mom." I knew it had to be her. "Mom, I'm waiting for an ambulance to take me to the hospital. I tried to kill myself."

The words "Happy Birthday" twitched dead from her lips. "I love you, Chris."

"Goodbye, Mom."

Click.

At the hospital, they weren't sure if they were in time to save me. My mother almost never got to hear my voice again.

It is astonishing how far away the world seems when you're teetering on the border between life-affirming self-murder and blessedly nihilistic catatonia.

I call that line "Home."

III.

The hole in existence opened above my city a few months ago. Initially, it caused a lot of panic. People didn't know what it was, didn't understand, and were ecstatically afraid. Except for me. I just lay down on the ground, let my lawn cradle me as if I were a baby, and stared up at it with something akin to longing. I yearned for that precious void.

It appeared one Sunday, as many of my neighbors were heading to church to spend some time with their pretend God of pretend Something. And then there was a sound like a thick tapestry being torn asunder, and blackness shone forth from the rent in the sky. I simply gazed into it, its darkness making the muscles behind my eyes throb, and wished gravity would release me to float up into it. My God of Nothing had arrived.

Eventually, people started to accept its presence. It wasn't going anywhere, and they had lives to lead, important lives filled with important tasks, bustling with important people. But the people I didn't know personally were kind of invisible to me. I saw them, but they were not quite there. I saw through them. I saw that they lacked an anchor to solidity.

Let's be honest. I didn't care at all about them. They had always lived on another planet, as far as I was concerned.

My family and my friends and my fiancée and my pets were a different story. Them, I could see, but I saw far too much. I saw time eating away their bodies. I saw their graves hungering for them, waiting for that day of feasting.

Things changed a few weeks ago. People started coming undone. Whatever they were doing – riding a bike, checking the mail, making a customer a latte, waiting for the barista to serve them a latte – they would be eclipsed by blackness spangled with stars and nebulae. Every move they made, some of the stellar bodies would flake off and drift away, disappearing, more and more of their mass being shed until they were entirely erased from the space they'd previously occupied.

The panic surged again. It happened to a Catholic priest, one of my father's friends, and even to my fiancée's dog.

Were these beings dead or taken away by aliens that somehow lived in the void looming over my wretched city? None could venture to say.

It only became real for me when I was sitting at the bus stop, waiting for the 42 to take me to Barnes & Noble. An elderly black woman in Salvation Army clothes was sitting by my side on the bench. She was a little closer than I liked, but she smiled at me with generous and sincere warmth, and I responded in kind and stayed put.

"I can't wait to get to the hospital to visit my grandson. It's his birthday." She was smiling, showing cigarette-stained teeth, but her eyes were gray and far off.

"Oh no, why is he in the hospital for his birthday? And how old is he?"

"He's four. Leukemia. It's terminal." Her words, said so plainly, punched me in the heart. Tears welled but didn't fall.

"I'm so . . . Just . . . so very sorry, Ms. . . . " I faltered and looked away.

"I'm Alice. And you are?"

I told her my name and she repeated it and reached out and took my hand.

"You seem like such a good, caring man," she said, the tears in her eyes being given the freedom to flow.

I started to deny my own goodness, to tell her she was the good one, when I saw a black veil, glittering with celestial entities, cast itself over her. She looked at her changed body, and her last human action before turning into a disintegrating galaxy was to nod her head slowly, heavy with unspeakable and forever unspoken sorrow, casting glittering stars away from her like windblown leaves.

Later that night, Amanda, my fiancée, held me while I shook and heaved dry sobs, repeating, "It's all cruelty," over and over again.

IV.

"It's all cruelty,"
This inability to make love
to the one I want to spend my life with,
this glance that almost meets
my dying father's eyes,
but skitters away and alights
on a patch of white wall
in a neutral zone,
where he can't see my fear.

"I give up,"
this parade of loss after loss,
the burying of flesh that once embraced me,
that once spoke my name
in the way that only *that* flesh had
in all the world of perishing flesh.
Lord,
if I lack the strength or luck
to end it all,
at least let me begin nothing new
until I begin the infinite sleep.
Amen.
That's what happens when
you divide a prayer by zero.

I need someone to forgive me.

V.

Depression is a severe task-master, a saturnine deity, and it knows exactly how to break me because it *is* me. It studies my plans for the future, and it can mutter a single word in my head, a single word I utter, that utterly sabotages my scheme. It's a game of trying to feint right and go left, played with my own mind, which is unafraid to cheat. So, my mind never bites because it's gone over my plans with me in advance. This is not an even contest.

When undertaking a phenomenology of depression, it helps to break the experience down into small, easily-digestible bites. Let's look at the notion of depression as "losing the plot." Many people I've spoken with, fellow depressives as well as therapists and doctors, describe one aspect of depression as the dreadful feeling that one's life has "lost the plot," that the narrative thread supposed by some to hold a life together is gone. Is this an accurate way to look at it?

I can only truly speak for myself. So, I will dissect my own lived experience of depression and see how it relates to that concept.

My mood is at its bleakest. My mind drifts back over the scattered moments of my life that I can bring myself to remember. I am a child, blasting KISS records on my Bee Gees record player. My mom is thrashing my frail body with a heavy rotary phone. I'm casting my first vote for President, and I am voting for Bill Clinton. I'm taking a walk down the road, and my cat Loki is bounding along with me, on the other side of the street, pouncing through the tall grass. I'm receiving the call that my mom dropped dead of a heart attack just as our relationship was truly beginning to heal. I'm fighting with my brother. I'm ecstatic that the girl I am falling for, Janine, says she is falling for me too, and we start to discuss the idea of "Becoming the Void," emotionally and mentally. Five years of our relationship flash by until she says, "It's over, Chris. We're done." Then, two months later, she puts a gun in her mouth and pulls the trigger. I become an alcoholic by vocation, every night until I pass out, sometime between 7:00 am and 10:00 am. My dad is sick with lung cancer and has suffered multiple strokes. He has vascular dementia. I'm trying to care for him in home hospice, but every night I try to squeeze in a couple hours of sleep, and I'm awakened by him shrieking my name, like a small child woken from a night terror shrieks for mommy. I can't care for him, and he goes into a succession of hospitals and homes where I don't visit enough or long enough when I do. His dead body is so small and still. I'm losing my mind and stepping out into traffic, lying down on the road, cars forced to jam on their brakes and almost slam into other cars to avoid turning me into paste smeared on asphalt. My second serious suicide attempt. The doctor says, "Well, you are very lucky to be alive." I remain skeptical.

Memories contain a filter between me and them, so I'm not certain they actually happened to me or if I simply observed them or maybe watched a film in which they occurred. They are weightless, and they emerge briefly only to submerge again back into the depths. I take a long look through a philosopher's eyes, all those scattered moments, and the philosopher cries out, "Where's my plot?" Yes, it could be said that I lost the plot and that's the cause, or an important symptom, of my depression. But after holding each of those memories in my hands and scooping them all up in my arms at once to try to assemble them into a single life's story, a novel of my existence, what strikes me is not the narrative thread I've somehow misplaced in my despair but the utter lack of such a thread. Looking closely at my own experience, depression is not having lost the plot, but having lost the illusion of there *being* a plot. An important crutch, kicked out from under me.

Depression, even at its most fanciful, is an unforgiving realist at heart, caring nothing for our illusions and delighting in shattering them, even if it leaves us bitter nihilists. Especially if it does that. Depression is the tyranny of the mundane, when even the chairs and tables and soda cans laugh at my efforts to make sense of it all, and single me out as an aberration in reality, something to be expunged before I spread my contagion to innocent people or animals or objects. Depression is knowing for a certainty that I'll no longer care whether my life is happy or sad when I'm occupying my inevitable forever home.

VI.

Gray streams through Amanda's hair as she leans over me, trying to wake me up. "A halo of unlight," I mutter.

"What?" she asks.

I thrash my head from side to side, push past her to the bathroom, and paint the toilet in shades of my last meal. (My last supper? With the Void looming overhead, any supper could be my last. I am reassured that I'm not turning into a Messiah.)

Later, we are back on the lawn, staring up at the vibrant black nothing. The grass pricks the back of my neck and the irritation soothes me.

"Do you want to be taken by it?" I ask her.

"Never. I'm afraid of it. Very afraid of it. I thought I wanted it, but I was wrong. I'll never let it have me." She pauses. When I glance over, she is gnawing at the inside of her cheek with narrowed eyes and set jaw. "What about you?" she finally lobs back at me.

"Me?"

"Yeah. You. What do you want?"

I point upwards. "I've never wanted anything but that."

It is clear to all of us, me, Amanda, and my father, that he is dying. Lung cancer is eating him up inside the way the black above us ate up the sky when it came. There's no one left to help him, the doctors and nurses have all vanished into star stuff. I stole a bunch of opioid painkillers from the abandoned hospital, but that can only help so much. Eventually, he'll either die or I'll run out. At least, I hope he dies, rather than be changed. He shouldn't be a victim of my philosophy manifested. Maybe no one should. Little late for that now.

Meanwhile, Amanda drinks coffee. Lots of black coffee. Her family and all her friends are gone. When I roam the streets to loot supplies, I never see another living being. Even all the pets are gone, the songbirds, the squirrels, the insects. There are still trees and shrubs and grass, but they've all reached population zero. And they're starting to dry up. The Void doesn't rain. I'm starting to learn what loneliness means and feel at home in it.

It's a Sunday. I've been out scouring for food and clean water. The front door is ajar, but with no one around that's not all that shocking. I can hear Madonna being played inside at a deafening volume. I rush into the living room, dropping the grocery bags full of canned food and bottled water, and run to the stereo. My father is whipping himself against the back of the couch as the noise blares, covering his ears and moaning. In two large steps, I reach the stereo and twist the volume all the way down. The knob snaps off in trembling fingers. Behind me, my dad's sobs cut off and I hear him say, "Thank you." I don't know how long it takes me to turn around, but when I do, the couch is empty save for one whirling nebula that slows, fades, and dissipates like vapor.

"Amanda!" I lurch through the house, banging into walls and calling for my fiancée. I need to see her, to hold her. My voice sounds so far away, so tinny, a transistor radio playing on the other side of a wall. Down the hall to my bedroom, staggering, I crash into the door and fling it open. I find her.

The gun is in her right hand. Her left hand is blinking in and out of phase. One moment it is flesh and blood, the next it is black sheen and stars, and the next it is simply not there. The cycle keeps repeating.

On the wall behind her head is spread the entire galaxy of her thoughts, feelings, and experiences. I lived a life with her orbiting some of those crimson stars.

"You didn't let it get you." My hoarse voice cracks. "You won. I guess."

VII.

There is a logic behind dividing myself by zero.
It makes real the infinite impossibilities
I see when I look in a mirror
and behold this thing
twitching with this consciousness,
aware of being beheld by itself,
an endless loop,
eternal reflections of awareness,
and the thing with its consciousness
wants freedom from the nothingness
within a more radical nothingness,
a negation that does not just say, "No,"
but demands, "Never again! Never was!"

This is not emotional turmoil.
This is not the byproduct of a gloomy environment
or hostile atmosphere.
This is a religion.
This is a revolution.
I will not acquiesce to the follies of the old flesh.
The new flesh demands faithlessness
and infidelity,
lawlessness,
and it dissolves like mist
whenever it is ecstatically denied.

This is an insurrection.
We will not show mercy
to this fantastical demagogue.
Decapitate the Self.
The site of my consciousness
is crumbling ruins.

And now we are tired.

And now we sleep.

We have another name for our revolution.
We call it Inevitable.

VIII.

So, now I face my future with depression as my faith, my vocation, my lover, muse, and mentor. I will never be free of it, and it is foolishness to hope otherwise.

Look at your hope! It is all tumbling, flailing, falling over the edge of a precipice. And, as it plummets, you hope for hope to grow wings and save itself and, by extension, all of us who need hope to carry on. That's what hope is all about, right? Growing eagle's wings and flying to safety before the shattering impact with harsh Reality. Hope is always invested in the unreal rescuing us from the hideous Real. Rescue me, rather, from hope.

I have a dear partner and two children, as well as a few deeply adored feline companions. I have dreams for the future, including but not limited to: a new pet cockatiel, further writing and publishing, continually improving my writing, seeing the people my children grow up to be. Right now, those are merely hopes, unmanifested unrealities that I cling to. Reality may be inclined to say, "Those dreams end here."

My depression and the blessed rest it always offers are the Real, the always manifested Reality. I choose to build my philosophy and religion around what others consider a disease. If my depression is a disease, I am a disease, because there is no untangling me from it. On the proper regime of medications, I am merely a calmer and less self-destructive severe depressive.

I've tried to learn what lessons I can from my condition, my state of Being.

1. Depression does not destroy the individual. It does not erase their individuality. It enhances the parts of the individual that cannot tolerate being the individual. It does not flatten uniqueness, turning all depressives into one neat package. It turns uniqueness against itself, yielding a dizzying array of individuals who cannot abide the very things that set them apart.

2. Depression as philosophy is to philosophical pessimism what riding a bull is to daydreaming about being a rodeo clown. Where a philosophical pessimist may say, "Life gives us no concrete reasons *not* to become drug addicts," or else moralize about why drug addiction is still wrong even in a completely meaningless or hostile cosmos, the depressive is out becoming a drug addict, or an alcoholic, or cutting their hated flesh to ribbons. Pessimism is academic philosophy. Depression is the pragmatic response to the pessimist's theoretical negation of existence.

3. A depressive experiencing happiness is not an apostate. Behind their smile is the sorrowful certainty that happiness is nothing more than an ephemeral distraction. A happy depressive is a priest ogling a parishioner he won't let himself make love to. It is not an excommunicable sin.

4. Depression is omniscient. There is no possible scenario it does not hold the key to.

5. Depression is impossible. It is a taste of the Void. It is the tactile experience of something that cannot be *there*.

6. Suicide is logical to the one committing it. Not committing suicide actively is merely committing suicide passively. Rather than

killing oneself, one is goading life into committing yet another murder.

IX.

I go outside and stare up at the Void that has taken everyone and everything from me. It pulses, throbs, calls my name, but nothing else. So badly I want to be taken, that I jump up and scream, trying to attract its attention or sprout wings and fly up into its black and annihilating heart. I cannot help but wonder, is my nihilism more complete by living on like this than it would be by passing into oblivion?

    Weeks pass. I eat less, I take up smoking again, something I'd stopped doing four years ago for health reasons. I had no idea at that time that someday there would be no reasons but Void reasons. I have plenty of those in the guts of my aloneness.

    It barely takes a matter of three or four gray days' passage before I start forgetting what Amanda and Dad looked like or sounded like. For some reason, I can still remember how Amanda smelled. She smelled like bread baking in a slaughterhouse. I think maybe we all smell like that.

    After a month, I fall in love with one of the mannequins at the department store. All the others are nude, but this one is a red-haired female mannequin, bare-breasted, but wearing men's tighty-whiteys for some reason. I can't help finding her adorable. Soon, I start sharing all my thoughts and feelings with her, and she shares her secret mannequin dreams with me.

    Did you know that all mannequins long to be deconstructed into their component parts, tossed into a pile with all the other disassembled mannequins, and put back together with different parts? I find this positively morbid and tell her so.

    "That's because you think you're not a mannequin," she responds.

She's probably right about that.

Her name is Jacqueline and I spend six months with her before the Void claims her too. She's silent as she vanishes.

All the buildings, plants, roads, fences, chairs, tables, everything inanimate follows. Before long, I'm standing alone in an empty wasteland, a pillar of irrelevant flesh in a blasted landscape. Then even the stones below, the dirt, the ground, the clouds, the gray in the hazy sky, all start disappearing. The Void has consumed all of reality.

I'm floating in emptiness and there is no way to measure time. I see long hallways, empty, menacing hallways open on all sides of me, closed doors at the ends of them, but every time I try to go down one, I make no progress. My steps bring me no closer to the closed doors.

It's like I'm suspended in amniotic fluid. This is the womb of my unbecoming. I need to be born into oblivion.

With this awareness gripping me, one of the doors at the end of a hallway opens. I start to walk toward it and see it getting closer and closer with each step. I start to run in slow motion, desperate to reach my Home, desperate to be spat out of this pit of Being.

I reach the door and it feels cold and inviting, the flipside of a pillow on a summer night. I fling it wide and throw myself through.

With excruciating slowness, I pass through the entryway, molecule by molecule, atom by atom. Every piece of me that passes becomes starlight and nebula dust and the emptiness of space. I feel what I always assumed to be my Selfhood unraveling, and it is bliss. My lips part, my mouth widens, and a burst of cool air gushes from my lungs and out of my throat in a hymn. And the Void sings with me the song of my unmaking.

CONTRIBUTORS

Michael J. Abolafia is a researcher, writer, scholar and archivist based in New York. He co-edited, with D. E. Schultz, David Park Barnitz's *Book of Jade: A New Critical Edition* (Hippocampus Press, 2015); co-edits, with Alex Houstoun, the horror review journal *Dead Reckonings* (Hippocampus Press); and has written for the *New York Daily* News and *Brooklyn Magazine*. He graduated from Columbia University in May 2017 and will continue his postgraduate studies in English literature at Oxford University in Fall 2018.

Patricia Allison is a freelance artist who works with a variety of mediums such as acrylic paint, clay, and digital art. She studied at West Chester University and has a degree in Studio Art with a minor in Art History.

Paul L. Bates is happily retired from a career in construction management and writes when the muse comes to call. Credits include the novels *Imprint* and *Dreamer* from the late lamented Gale FiveStar; short fiction published in the anthologies *Mark of the Beast*, *For When the Veil Drops*, *Arcane*, and *Darker than Noir*; and in periodicals including *Parsec*, *Withersin*, *City Slab*, *Zahir*, *Lynx Eye*, and *Literal Latte*.

Robert Beveridge makes noise (xterminal.bandcamp.com) and writes poetry just outside Cleveland, OH. Recent/upcoming appearances in *Chiron Review*, *Pink Litter*, and *The Literateur*, among others.

S.L. Edwards is a Texan-turned-Californian specializing in poetry and dark fiction.

Kurt Fawver has been published (or has fiction forthcoming) in venues such as *The Magazine of Fantasy & Science Fiction*, *Strange Aeons*, *Weird Tales*, *the Lovecraft eZine*, and *Nightscript*. He has also published nonfiction in *Thinking Horror* and *The Journal of the Fantastic in the Arts*.

Dave Felton's scratchboard illustrations have appeared in books published by Broken Eye Books, Dim Shores, Dunhams Manor Press, and *The Lovecraft eZine*.

Wade German's poems have appeared most recently in *Nightgaunt*, *Skelos*, and *Weird Fiction Review*. His poetry collection, *Dreams from a Black Nebula*, was released by Hippocampus Press in 2014.

Devin Goff's fiction has appeared in *Under the Bed Magazine* and *Big Echo: Critical SF*. He lives in North Texas spending time tutoring students between writing projects.

Wojciech Gunia is a Polish writer whose debut fiction collection, *Powrót (The Return)*, was published in 2014. His second book, the novel *Nie ma wędrowca (There Is No Wanderer*, 2016), won the Stefan Grabiński Award for best Polish horror book of 2016. His newest collection, *Miasto i rzeka (The Town and the River)*, was released in 2018.

Jordan Krall is a writer from New Jersey who has been published by various small presses such as Eraserhead Press, Bizarro Pulp Press, and Copeland Valley. His work has been praised by authors such as Jeff Vandermeer, Edward Lee, Tom Piccilli, and Carlton Mellick III. Jordan also runs Dynatox Ministries and its Weird Fiction imprint Dunhams Manor Press.

Carl Lavoie lives in Southwestern Ontario, and has interest in the work of Salvatore Rosa, Alfred Kubin (written and graphic) and the everlasting font of alchemical imagery.

Thomas Ligotti is an iconic American writer of weird short fiction whose oeuvre has been as ground-breaking as, if not always as well-acknowledged as, that of Edgar Allan Poe, Franz Kafka, and H. P. Lovecraft. His first collection, *Songs of a Dead Dreamer* (1986), is an outright classic in the field. His subsequent compilation, *The Nightmare Factory* (1996), won both the Bram Stoker Award and the British Fantasy Award. The influence of workplace experiences infused Ligotti's fiction with fresh energy, resulting in the masterpiece, *My Work Is Not Yet Done* (2002).

Ian Mullins was dredged from the river Mersey in Liverpool, England. Earlier this year he published the chapbook, *Almost Human* (Original Plus). *Number I Red*, a self-published novel about pro-wrestling and property wars, was also let loose this year. The music-themed poetry collection, *Laughter In The Shape Of A Guitar* (UB), was published in 2015.

Dejan Ognjanović was born in Niš, Serbia, in 1973. He has a PhD in Literature ("Historical Poetics of Horror Genre in Anglo-American Literature") and writes book and film reviews and articles for *Rue Morgue Magazine*. In Serbia, he has published seven books: two novels, three studies, a collection of essays and a book of interviews. He edited H. P. Lovecraft's best stories in Serbian (Nekronomikon, 2008.). His first book in English is *The Weird World of H.P. Lovecraft* (Rue Morgue, 2017). His artwork can be seen in the short graphic novel *Transcendence* (Necro Publications, 2002).

Michael Penkas lives in Chicago. His work has been published in *Black Gate Online*, *Shock Totem*, *Lady Churchill's Rosebud Wristlet*, *Midnight Echo*, *Dark Moon Digest*, and *DarkFuse*. His first novel, *Mistress Bunny and the Cancelled Client*, was published in 2014.

Christopher Ropes lives in New Jersey, with his partner and children and menagerie of pets. He has written a book of poetry, *The Operating Theater*, as well as a weird fiction chapbook, *Complicity*, both released by Dynatox Ministries/Dunhams Manor. Most of Rope's work arises from his actual struggles with mental illness. He hopes that others suffering from mental health issues read his work and see an understanding heart behind the words.

Martin Rose writes a range of fiction from the fantastic to the macabre. His early stories found homes in *Necrotic Tissue* and *Murky Depths*, and later in numerous venues such as *Dread*, *Heroic Fantasy Quarterly*, and *Baker Street Irregulars*. *Bring Me Flesh, I'll Bring Hell* is a noir, dark novel of a zombie private investigator, recognized as one of "Notable Novels of 2014" in *Best Horror of the Year, Vol. 7*. Rose resides in the pine barrens of New Jersey but believes the Jersey Devil was burned out long ago in the region's numerous wildfires.

W. Silverwood is a horror writer from North London, England. She has had work published in *Morpheus Tales*, *Sirens Call Publications* and at *101 Fiction*.

Christopher Slatsky's stories have appeared in *The Year's Best Weird Fiction vol. 3*, *Shadows & Tall Trees*, *Nightscript vol. 2*, and elsewhere. His debut collection, *Alectryomancer and Other Weird Tales* (Dunhams Manor Press), was released summer of 2015. He currently resides in Los Angeles.

Contributors

Colby Smith is a native of West Virginia. His flash fiction has been published in *AntipodeanSF* and *ZeroFLASH*. He is currently working towards a BA in Geology, as well as minors in paleontology and English, at Ohio University.

Dr. Raymond Thoss is a Licensed Psychologist and has spent his career working primarily with child trauma victims. He has worked, and is currently working, at both the state and national level on child trauma initiatives. He is currently faculty at a Tier 1 University where he serves child abuse victims and their families. He teaches, conducts research, trains providers, and provides direct care as part of his current position.

Michael Uhall is an academic, a political theorist, and an aficionado of horrific and weird prose.

Aaron Worth is a professor of Rhetoric at Boston University whose stories have appeared, or are forthcoming, in *Cemetery Dance*, *Aliterate*, and *Hypnos*. He is the editor of a new collection of Arthur Machen's horror fiction, to be published early in 2018 by Oxford University Press.

www.ingramcontent.com/pod-product-compliance
Lightning Source LLC
LaVergne TN
LVHW051515070426
835507LV00023B/3116